WHY MEN LIE

WHY MEN LIE

REMOVING THE WEB OF LIES COVERING TRUTH

Samuel Lamanna

Winner's Circle C&S

Contents

Dedication

This book is dedicated to my best friend and wife Cynthia, who has borne the scars of my growth into manhood and now is enjoying the rewards of me becoming the man I am today. In her own words she has said, "I married potential". I've also heard her say, "I don't have time to break in another man".

Without her, none of this would be possible. She is my inspiration, the one who paid the price when it meant the most, and the one who deserves my full recognition and love. Her wisdom and creativity are matched by no one. She is the kindest and most beautiful person I know. I will love you always.

To my daughter Victoria, who dedicated countless hours to help me with this book while following her dreams. Her passion and diligence have helped make this possible; and will come in handy as a new mom. I love you.

To my son Rjay, who continues to remind me of the man I have become. He keeps encouraging me to be better and to always keep growing. He is more of a man than I could ever hope to be. I'm very proud of you and love you.

To my son-in-law Christian, who challenged me to remain a changed man when he decided to date my daughter. A great husband and now father.

To my new grandson Charlie, who has touched my heart deeply by his arrival. May the lessons I have learned be ingrained in your heart and life to become the man you were meant to be. Your infectious smile continues to melt my heart each day. I love you a lot.

To my new granddaughter Sophia. You are so beautiful and special. We knew your name before your parents decided on it. We know that you will do great things in life. Holding you in my arms I can tell you will keep everyone on their toes. I love you dearly.

To all our future family both known and unknown. I pray the principles of this book guide you to be true.

To all my other friends who have been my lifelong support, thank you.

Without any of you, this work would not be possible.

Samuel (Honest) Lamanna III

Warning!

WARNING!
READING THIS BOOK MAY CAUSE YOU TO TELL THE TRUTH.

If you lie, have lied, know someone who lies, or have been hurt by lies then this book is for you.

If you haven't realized it yet by this book's title (Why Men Lie), in this book I often mention men. Don't let that bother you. Men may refer to father's, brothers, husbands, and everyone else on earth- All Mankind. I often single out men in particular because that's what I see when I look in the mirror every day. I also spent years helping men improve their lives and relationships.

The principles in this book apply to everyone and anyone who lies or has had to deal with someone who does. The principles shared in this book have come from years of study, counseling people, and personal reflection.

Most of the names used in these stories have been changed, some have not. All the personal stories are true. I hope you enjoy them all.

I'm hoping that from reading this book you will be inspired

to pursue truth and forsake a life of lies. That you would be honest with yourself and others, and no longer be a liar. Presenting Why Men (Mankind) Lie (Lies).

Samuel grew up in a little town near the capital of New York. There was little warmth there to be found. Most months of the year were cold. His childhood was filled with the optimism of a dreamer. He would daydream in school and whenever he had the time. A handful of happy memories filled his thoughts, surrounded by the fantasies he often added. Samuel needed to dream. It kept him from the reality that was going on around him.

He imagined a father that was actively involved in his life. One that cared about his daily activities and loved being with him. A mother that found joy in her family and the future they were building together. Close siblings that could talk about anything and were nearly inseparable. Nothing was farther than the truth. There was little warmth there. His home was as cold as it was outside.

This fantasy he thought was a lie. The truth corresponded to something more like this: A father that merely resembled a picture on the wall. You knew he was there. He was so quiet and absent from your life that you often forget that he existed, except when he got angry. You had to hide. A mother who was trapped in a cycle of endless relational despair, longing for us to find something better. Siblings, through a survival-like mindset, were consumed with fighting and finding their escape.

So, Samuel dreamed. He made his own reality with lies. It crept in so deep, and the pain hurt so much that it filled his dreams with nightmares. The nightmares were dark and ominous. They became a nightly ritual. This optimistic kid, who others saw on the outside, hid a lie deep within. Suicidal nightmares were repeated every night. For him, there seemed to be no escape. Fear gripped his life and death seemed so close. He was spiraling down a deep dark hole.

No one knew this struggle to survive was going on within him. Dark thoughts and dreams told him lies he believed. They seemed to be winning, but this fight was not over. He encountered something more powerful than lies and darkness. Light and Truth. Surrendering to the light, he realized God was his true father. It was a hope that shone through the thick darkness. A new day emerged. An awakening that pierced the night and took away the hopelessness he felt within.

Reborn into a new person, he vowed to never lie to himself again. He would now make it his mission to seek the truth at any cost. Growing up he was named after two other generations of Samuels. The first two Samuels, his father and grandfather, were given middle names. This Samuel was not. Even though his parents never officially gave him a middle name, he had one waiting for him. A name that would reveal his life's true purpose and who he was meant to become would now define him. His new middle name would be "Honest."

This began a lifelong journey. A fresh new perspective for Sam. Having faced what seemed like a near-death experience, he no longer viewed things in his life the same way.

After graduating high school, he joined the Army National Guard with a desire to give back to his country. He then decided to attend college, on the opposite side of the country, where he earned a bachelor's degree. Sam married his high school sweetheart. Starting a new family, he became a father to two wonderful children. He earned income as a delivery driver for UPS until one painful day everything changed. Following a decade of hard work, an injury sent him in a completely new direction. Sam repurposed himself and became a real estate broker and investor. This endeavor had many highs and lows financially and emotionally.

Sam decided to take a "business break" and do something new to help others. He became a certified substance abuse counselor, which he enjoyed for several years before assuming a role as an investment counselor. During this time, he launched a nonprofit organization to help those in need.

When he was a rehab counselor, the ideas for this book emerged. This book is a culmination of the principles he learned while helping people become their best selves. Knowing the impact lies had on his own life, he desired to help his clients find freedom from their painful lifestyles. He was surrounded by people who told and believed lies. It became his mission in life to understand the impact their behaviors and choices had on themselves and their loved ones.

Samuel "Honest" Lamanna III

Introduction: Why Men Lie

We live in a society where truth seems lost. In the current environment of relativity, we have begun to redefine the very concepts and words that laid our foundation for understanding truth. Redefining words to mean what we want them to mean slowly seems to cause absolutes to disappear from our language. Yet they are still there.

Controlling communication and language may appear to dissolve absolutes, but they cannot disappear. We can personally deny the truth, but the truth will always confront our lives with what's real.

The tightrope walker may believe that they are no longer limited to the absolute truth of gravity, but it still is there.

The addict may believe that another high is just another high while denying the reality that an overdose is secretly waiting in the shadows to expose a morbid truth.

A businessman may believe the lie that theft is not stealing but just borrowing money to get ahead.

A husband may believe the lie that just looking without touching is harmless and won't impact his vows.

College students may believe the lie that they are invincible and what has happened to others will never happen to them.

Women may believe the lie that their beauty is merely physical while allowing others to exploit them for personal pleasure.

Ministers may believe the lie that they have their life under full control while disconnected from those they are committed to protect, guide, and teach.

Politicians may believe the lie that they are representing their constituents, while they are pushing a version of utopian truth, far separating them from those they swore to represent.

A father may believe the lie that his children don't need him, causing them to struggle to find their own identity.

All these people have something in common. They believe lies.

Simply stated, a lie is something that is not true. A lie is a lie. It's something that is not true even if we believe that it is true temporarily. Deception is believing a lie to be true and hiding it. Everyone at some point in their life will eventually find out they have been deceived. It does not matter whether we deceived ourselves or it came from someone else. The beauty of truth is that it always has a way of exposing what is false. That's why it is true. Truth exposes the lie. Truth exposes Lies.

Someone can have faith in the truth or faith in a lie. Eventually, the truth will reveal itself. We can resist this revealing of truth by denying or rejecting it, but it is still there.

By adhering to lies, many people are suffering mentally, emotionally, and physically. They are completely in denial of what is true and have believed the lie!

Think about the amount of stress it takes to continue to believe a lie. It takes a lie to keep a lie going. A liar can only take so much mentally, emotionally, and physically before they become overwhelmed. With each new lie comes an added new layer of stress. Each lie adds weight to this metaphorical burden making it increasingly harder to bear. This only compounds the issue until something gives way or breaks.

Repeatedly, liars continue to overwhelm their life with lies and deception. Addicts while using substances are lying to themselves. It's practically impossible to maintain sanity and manage their life while continuing to use substances to cope.

Until the truth is finally accepted, there can be no peace. We can only deny what is true for so long before the impact on our life becomes evident. Accepting the truth is real and true peace. Although to some, the lie has become so real that they would disagree. How can they believe anything else? It usually takes a catastrophic event or crisis to open them up to what is true. There is a God-force of tremendous magnitude that is continually pulling us towards the truth. Like gravity it's always working to reveal what is true when truth is violated. Always exposing lies.

Truth does not hurt us directly. We often hurt ourselves by resisting the truth. Every time we fight against it, we get hurt. Our pain may be physical pain especially if we think we can physically fly like a bird when the truth says otherwise. If we think our will to control a substance is stronger than a substance, we will soon realize it is a lie. Many people have felt the excruciating pain of lies in their relationships. The pain of a broken heart from someone you loved feels worse than any other type of pain. Mental, emotional, and spiritual pain will also come from the struggle to deny truth.

Humans were never meant to lie or live a lie. Truth will always win because it is solid truth. It is steady. It is unwavering. It is always there. It can't be sent away. Truth is often a reflection of what we are meant to be yet sometimes who we are not. It keeps us honest. It is on point. It is headed in the right direction. Just like true north, it is a reminder of the direction we are going and tells us when we are lost. Where is your true north?

Believing a lifelong lie is like believing north is south and east is west. It just isn't true. Some people are more comfortable living a fantasy than a life of truth. Pretending something is true that you know for sure it is not, is a fantasy. There can be some comfort in pretending, especially when your reality is so messed up. Eventually, everyone at some point must face reality. Face the truth. What is your truth?

If your life is filled with lies, you may begin to realize at some point that you are heading the wrong way. Fantasy feels so good that you would rather stay disillusioned than face your real life. You violated your basic human instincts. It has become all twisted inside; lies instead of truth, darkness instead of light, and confusion instead of clarity. Regret begins to take over. The only way for regret to dissipate is to turn things around. Move away from a life of dark lies towards truth and the clarity of light. Are you ready to straighten things out and make a move towards "Truth"?

1

Man Has Lost His Way

Men have lost their true direction. Men have lost themselves. They have abandoned much of what it means to be a man and have accepted lies as a normal part of their life. "Man" used to be a title of honor, dignity, love, and respect. One that invoked chivalry for others. In society today, it's no wonder why some men are hated so much by others. They are not being real men and therefore, people are not seeing real men.

A man is not a "real man" just because he was born male. Many people live with someone who is male but never took on the responsibility to mature into true manhood. The fact remains that we have many males in our society, but few men. Who would want to be around an immature male who never grew up?

Someone who is not who they say they are, is not a real

man. Someone pretending to be something else is not a real man. Many men embody selfishness, egoism, and a sense of male chauvinism. A person who only thinks about themselves and their own needs is not a real man. Someone whose life is all about building up themselves is not a real man. Someone who thinks he is better than a woman is not a real man. This can be seen in how he talks, treats, and looks at her. He believed a lie and he has become a liar.

George Foreman is someone many people knew for his "George Foreman Grill". They were sold to millions of households across America. While many people remember his grill, they may not remember to whom he lost his title as a professional boxing champion. Tommy Morrison became the World Boxing Organization's heavyweight champion in June of 1993 by unanimous decision, defeating George Foreman by a couple points. Morrison would hold this title for just a few months before losing it to someone no one thought could beat him.

What was supposed to be an easy match for Tommy Morrison turned into a true "Rocky" moment for Mike Bentt. In October of 1993, Bentt managed to throw a combination that shook Morrison hard off his feet in the first round. Morrison was able to get back up in time to continue fighting. Bentt capitalized on this boxer being stunned. He dropped him a second time. Morrison mustered everything left within him to get back up again but stood no match for the overly determined Bentt. They knew that there was a three-knockdown rule in effect to win the championship.

With his eye on the prize, Bentt collected every ounce of energy within him to continue the fight until Morrison went down the third time. Bentt became the new World Boxing Organization's champion on that day.

What is interesting is that Mike Bentt was a professional boxer, yet boxing was never something he had a burning desire to do. He was living a lie. He never had a passion for the sport. Bentt was only a boxer to please his father who was trying to live vicariously through him.

Bentt once said that "boxers are the worst liars because they deny the truth. They deny pain all the time." He fought for survival, but not because he liked it. His desire to prove himself to his father and his mentors led him to win the heavyweight championship in 1993. One year later Herbie Hide knocked him out, becoming the new champion. Mike Bentt left the fight in an ambulance. He was in a coma for four months. It caused him brain damage. In an interview, he said that it was the best thing that ever happened to him. The best thing? How could it be the best thing? It was because he was living a lie and became that lie. He didn't want to be a boxer. The medical report freed him. After embracing the truth of who he wanted to be, he found what he really loved. Acting. He is currently a successful British-American actor. Mike Bentt has played roles in numerous films and television programs. When Bentt was a boxer, he was not only denying the physical pain that the sport caused him, but also the pain of living his life for someone else. This issue is not only a Mike Bentt problem. This is not even a boxer problem. This is a "man" problem.

So, why do men lie? You see, men are the worst liars of all because they have denied the truth. Men have literally missed the mark.

Truth is the center of who and what men are supposed to be.

Think of life as a dartboard. Truth is at the center of the bullseye. It is surrounded by lies that miss the mark. Every decision that men make is another dart thrown on the board. They can hit the center towards truth or fail to hit the mark. The result of missing is lies. Hitting the bullseye takes practice and skill. Sometimes when aiming for truth, you miss the mark because you haven't developed the necessary skills needed to embrace truth completely.

When men fail to be exactly who they are, they are a lie. When men do not accomplish all, they are meant to do in their life and for others, then they become a lie. Men who know who they are and what they're meant for are aiming for the bullseye of truth. In life, maturity comes from taking on responsibility and being truthful. As boys learn to accept emotional, social, mental, and relational responsibility they mature into men. In the process, they discover who they are and what they ultimately are meant to do. The process of pursuing truth and accepting responsibility helps define their life and mission.

Some men are content with lies. Their bad aim has caused them to wound themselves and those close to them, yet they still refuse to improve their aim. Men sometimes don't realize the scope of the impact their actions have on others. Maybe they just don't care.

Other men just don't know where to stand, epitomizing the saying, "If you stand for nothing you fall for everything." Fall and fail hard, they do. Failing or missing the mark is easy. It does not take much skill. On life's dartboard, you can throw as wildly as you want if you don't care about winning in life. It will not matter. It takes no skill to lose. If you don't want to play, you have already lost. Indifference makes no difference. There is no escaping being who you are.

Every man can develop the winning skill set needed in life. The skill developed through practice will hit the mark. While aiming, actions begin to unfold that benefit everyone influenced by this man. The benefits are overwhelming. When a man hits the mark in truth, he becomes a power to be reckoned with. A power that is not just for him alone, but also for the benefit of those near him. When he takes the aim, he was always meant to take, he develops the necessary skills to win in life. The result is a bullseye!

Questions for Self-Reflection

How would you define manhood?

Describe a time when you pretended to be someone you weren't.

Why did you pretend to not be yourself?

Are you doing what you want to do in life? Explain.

What have been the major lies in your life?

How much do you desire truth in your life?

What do you see as the biggest difference between a man and a "real man?"

What difference does it make in your life?

2

Protecting Their Ego

An overflowing ego paves the way for arrogance and is best friends with pride. Lying and pride go together quite well. There's a common theme between lying and pride.

There is a good pride in oneself and in one's country that places value in people that are equal with themselves. It's an honest view of oneself and others. This good pride gives us a sense of belonging and accomplishment. This is not the pride we are referring to at all.

When we become full of pride it takes a turn for the worse. No longer are we concerned for the value in others and all we think about is self. Our eyesight shifts from seeing the "significance" in others to being blinded through selfishness. "Self" becomes what is most important. This is how we move from good pride to bad pride. A proverb says, (bad) "pride goes before destruction and a haughty spirit before stumbling."

What kind of man values protecting his ego? A prideful one.

Arrogance always proceeds an inevitable fracture. Where you find pride or arrogance you will soon find something ready to break, or already broken. Self-loving behavior severs relationships by fracturing trust, value, and respect.

Pride is viewing yourself as having more value than others. It is associated with pomp, swelling, and majesty. There is quite a difference between a person of actual intelligence and someone who just thinks they're smarter than everyone else around them. I'm sure you have been around a man who thought his brain weighed much more than yours. Even if someone is more intelligent, their desire to make sure everyone else knows it is a byproduct of arrogance, not true intelligence.

Interestingly, the word "majesty" is also associated with pride. That is because often prideful people like to be surrounded by the attention and service of others. They come first and want others to realize they place second to them. If they had their way, everyone around them would be serving them. They have a desire to be a majestic king rather than an honest knight. Protecting a prideful point of view can lead to a host of lies all to defend their big ego.

Being in a relationship with an extremely proud man is difficult at best. His pride leaves his life riddled with fractured relationships, stressful business associations, and distant friendships.

While it may not appear this way at first, a partner who is more concerned with protecting his ego than preserving your relationship leaves little room for you and your needs in the relationship.

A man who lies to protect his ego has tunnel vision. He has a blind spot regarding how to treat others and has difficulty seeing their true value. His relationships are suffering. He is blind to what is right in front of him. He often lacks the emotional intelligence necessary to nurture intimate relationships.

He has placed himself on a pedestal built on lies. If only he could step back a few feet and see the bigger picture. Maybe then, before it's too late, he can save his relationships and save his family from himself. Save them from his lies. Pride not only blinds, but it also deafens. I remember working at a call center that had close cubicles. You could hear everyone next to you very well. This was not a place where you wanted to be near a prideful overly selfish person who didn't consider others.

I happened to be the "lucky one" who sat next to such an individual. He was so loud and boisterous it was hard to do my job. The customers on my phone line could hear him in the next cubicle. They made comments about how they could not believe someone could be so rude in a customer service position. They could hardly hear me over his grandeur. The worst part was that he did not know the negative impact he was having on those near him. He was blinded by his selfish ambition and deafened towards our subtle cues. I remember thinking, "Was there a way to get him to, see? To listen? To have him hear what we hear?" If he did, it would not only improve his social life but the quality of life of everyone around him. Maybe then, people would stop avoiding him and he wouldn't have to crave attention from others.

When our primary motive is consumed with protecting our ego, we are blind to the hurt we cause others. Socially smart people, who encounter this type of ego, tend to back away and create distance between themselves and this narcissist. The egoist is also deafened by the several warning signs and cues telling them to change their ways. There comes a point when we have not only believed the lie - but we have also become the lie. Our lies have become so ingrained into our thinking that we are trapped by them.

That proverb about pride and stumbling is true. A vicious cycle of lies leaves destruction and fractures.

"Oh, how the mighty have fallen" and they always do. The higher you put yourself in comparison to others, the farther you must fall.

What makes a man think he is better than someone else? Is it having more money? While having money frees you from some basic worries, it also adds some new worries of its own. It changes your net worth, but not your human worth. You are valuable regardless of your money. True value is found in things money can't buy. Health, love, faith, joy, and true friendships. Money can't buy these valuable things in life. It can only add or take away from them.

If I'm diagnosed with cancer, can I buy a new cancer-free body? No. I can use money for better treatment and more comfort. I can't pay someone to take away my illness.

Can I buy love? No, you can't. You may be able to buy sex. Sex and love are not the same.

How about faith? Does a man who lies to your face while trying to buy your loyalty earn your trust? How much money does it cost to trust someone? None, because trust is priceless.

Does money make you happy? Maybe it does temporarily. It does not give you joy. No amount of wealth can give you that internal sense of wellbeing and peace. Many wealthy people are depressed, suicidal, and suffering. They have no joy inside.

If they could, they would pay any price to immediately have internal joy.

What price can you place on close friendships and relationships? Those connections are priceless. If you can buy your friends, someone else can buy them back. Wealthy people appear to automatically have a lot of friends. Are those the type of friendships and connections you want? Those who like you for your money don't like you, they like your money. They are not interested in connecting with you, they just want a connection to your wealth. When your money is gone, so are they.

Health, love, faith, joy, and true friendships cannot be bought with any amount of money. Their value is too high. They can only be earned.

How about status? Does someone's status make them more important than others? Interestingly, we live in a current society that idolizes status but has no respect or honor. Why is that? It's because we have not separated responsibility from value. Different responsibilities come with higher status or occupation, like an executive, a policeman, the mayor, the governor, or even the president. If society does not respect these positions, then there will be repercussions. Likewise, if those who have been given these responsibilities disrespect their office, it will impede their ability to conduct their functions for the greater good. People will lose faith in their ability to lead and ultimately, they will fail.

Status is a position of responsibility, not value over others. Just because someone has an important position does not make them more important than you. It is what you do, not who you are. In other words, a politician or an actor is not more valuable or more important than I am as a human being. They simply have more value in their responsibilities and community.

Just because an NBA player excels in his ability and function to play basketball well does not make him a more valuable human being. He is, however, a valuable basketball player. Whether he chooses to be a positive or negative role model has nothing to do with his function in basketball. It has everything to do with the value he sees in others and himself. It's amazing to see those who have chosen to use their platform for a higher purpose and help others. They don't look over the heads of others. They look at them face-to-face as equals. They see the value in others and respect them. They are true men.

Money and status can't make you a better human. That would be like putting a new coat of paint on a car and expecting it to outperform other cars. It doesn't. It can't. A car is a car regardless of its paint color. If you upgrade the engine under the hood, watch what happens. We can add certain qualities deep within us that will help us excel. It helps us to perform as a better person, just like a rebuilt car.

We can have internal value and worth despite what's external. It's the inner value that brings true richness in life. It's purchasing things that money can't buy. It's the true foundation for all men everywhere. The value of true manhood.

It's Not Just Black and White

People are neither completely humble nor completely full of pride. Who they are is a composition of the choices they have made. Labeling someone as a humble person or a prideful person is not always black and white. It just does not work that way.

Think of a game of tug of war. Every choice you make is a tug of the rope in the direction of pride or humility. Rarely are decisions a complete pull of the rope to one side. More commonly, these choices are slight movements of the rope to one side or the other. You may not even realize which direction you are tugging the rope in until the game is almost lost. Men move along this mental tug of war. When they give in or resist their different thoughts, feelings, or actions, they are pulled back and forth.

The middle ground between the opposites of humility and pride is a large, gray zone. This is where a majority of choices reside. Few people are the full essence of pride or humility. Many people gradually move towards pride and lying so slowly that they don't realize how much they have changed over time. They look back and think, "I used to be different." People are constantly changing, whether it's for better or for worse.

Without being conscious of our thoughts, feelings, and actions, we may steadily change into someone we never anticipated. We may never see the consequences that are coming. There may be many red flags along this process. The more prideful we are the more we will not see them and will be blindsided. Exact consequences are rarely all spelled out but become clear and evident when we face them.

Life battles rarely face you directly straight on. That would be too easy to notice. It hits you from the side or from behind making it hard to see. Just like a lion crouching in the tall grass, stalking its prey, and waiting for the right moment to pounce. Often little consequences begin combining into bigger issues. While a definite cause and effect are happening, it is not always an immediate effect. We often don't see the consequences that each of our negative choices create until it's too late.

There is a domino effect that happens. It's a chain reaction where one event sets off a chain of other events. The domino pushed over, takes less energy than produced by the falling domino. It can push over a larger domino. In physics, this is called gravitational potential energy. The choices we make are like these individual dominos. While choices that cause severe consequences aren't always directly caused by the first domino or choice, it was that first domino that started the process. Often little decisions push over larger unexpected consequences because they are part of a process of choices made previously. This makes a cumulative effect for consequences to follow. The potential for failure is greater with each negative decision that is made. When someone drinks and drives, they are usually not choosing to get a DWI, go to rehab, lose their family, or kill someone. These choices are a direct result of multiple poor choices and repeated negative behaviors. It starts with thinking incorrect thoughts, enjoying wrong feelings, treating others poorly, and not thinking of others. In every incorrect thought, emotion, and action manipulation helps you to slowly and surely self-destruct. It is within every thought, emotion, and action where the tension lies. The tension between truth and error. Right and wrong. This is also where we change and how we grow. This is a key for self-improvement, but a spiritual transformation is necessary as a catalyst for continual change.

We cannot do this alone. We all need help at one time or another. Once we have identified our problem this is only the beginning of the resolution. We must be mindful of every thought, emotion, and action. What are we feeding in our thought life?

What are we starving? What we feed in thought and emotion will grow in meditation. What we meditate on will grow into action. Our actions become habits. Habits become lifestyles.

If I am prone to lying to protect my ego, then I need to work on being truthful and humble. This can start by saying, "I am sorry." Admitting you are wrong. Embrace the truth. True humility means you are willing to accept others' help and advice. Do this and you have taken the first step in identifying your issue and admitting your shortcomings. It does not stop there. You will need to continue to reinforce positive thoughts, emotions, and behaviors for change to set in for the long term.

Glue has many applications that are beneficial to mankind, but not all glue is the same especially in woodworking. Two of the most common glues in carpentry are wood glue and Cyanoacrylate (CA), otherwise known as superglue. There is a big difference between superglue and wood glue. Superglue creates a chain bond between the two components glued together. Although it dries fast and has a hardened bond it is not permanent. It is super-fast drying and super-strong. It lasts as long as you don't hit it with something hard; breaking the chain that connects it together. Hitting something hard that has been super glued can easily fracture and break because it lacks flexibility. Wood glue, on the other hand, is more permanent than superglue. It does not create a temporary chain-bond. Instead, it seeps into the wood pieces that are being glued together, becoming a part of the wood itself.

Men often appear to have changed their behaviors and attitudes, but they have only superglued their change and it is temporary. It may appear that they have changed, but when life throws something difficult their way, it becomes clear that it was not lasting. Things just fall apart. Men often choose this method of change because it is easier and a quick fix. They simply just want the current situation causing them stress to change. They want the relationship to improve quickly. They want it fixed now. They want others to notice their fake transformation right away. This quick-fix attitude of wanting to get back to "the way things were" won't last. The superglue bond, though it appears strong, has not become a part of who he really is. The change we are seeing is actually a superficial lie.

Men need to take the long road to change. This process is like using wood glue to reinforce this change. Wood glue permanently bonds to the wood and becomes a part of the wood being glued together. It creates the flexibility and permanent solution that is needed. Yes, it takes much longer to set and harden. When it is completed, you become a completely new man. A true man.

This reinforcement can be done by reminding yourself of what is true and resisting what is wrong. You must consider the strength of the negative forces pulling you back to pride and to your old lies. This will help to determine the time and strength that is needed for this "new you" to remain changed. Clamps are behaviors or standards that are personally applied. They help make these changes last. They remove the pressure to fall back into old habits. These clamps are what give your new mindset time to resist the force of your old habits. They consist of behaviors that may seem a bit extreme to others who do not share your exact same standards.

A person who has had a problem with being arrogant for many years will be faced with more challenges to change than someone who has moments of pride. A man who lied once will not have the same trouble as the man who lived his life filled with lies. The man who continuously pushed others down to get ahead will need more reinforcement to change than the man who just thought he was better than someone else. The pressure to conform to old habits and mindsets is strong. It will require some extreme behavioral adjustment while the metaphorical "glue" takes the time it needs to harden your new change, mindset, or beliefs. In time, the clamps can be removed as long as the glue to your new mindset has hardened.

A man who acknowledges that he has a problem with lying and pride has a chance to change. Remember, it's not the outward changes we are looking for, but the inward ones. Changes in thought, emotion, affection, and eventually changed action. Someone willing to embrace extreme behaviors to keep them from the negative pull of their past may see real change. A spiritual awakening comes from embracing this kind of truth. This helps you to grow. Don't you want to be who you were meant to be? A man of truth.

Believing A Lie Is Nothing New

During the 1840s until the 1860s, the world saw many advancements along with many struggles. There was much political upheaval, social reforms, and scientific advancements. It was a time of much uncertainty but was continuously sprinkled with hope. Charles Dickens, in his 1859 historic novel, got it right. In "The Tale of Two Cities", he wrote, "It was the best of times, it was the worst of times, it was the age of wisdom, it was the age of foolishness, it was the epoch of belief, it was the epoch of incredulity, it was the season of light, it was the season of darkness, it was the spring of hope, it was the winter of despair, we had everything before us, we had nothing before us, we were all going direct to heaven, we were all going direct the other way."

This era was consumed with many solutions and many obstacles. Many lies were being infiltrated into society. Many truths were being ignored or embraced. Technology has begun making the world a bit smaller than it used to be. Just like locomotives paved the way for people everywhere to move farther and faster; technology, science, and civil unrest continued onward.

A new Pope took office disregarding what the last one believed; that trains and gas lights were a sure path to hell. Walter Hunt invented the safety pin to pay off a fifteen-dollar debt he owed a friend. He sold the patent to a company for four hundred dollars not realizing its full potential. The company that he sold this to made millions of dollars off his patent. Samuel Morse, one of the inventors of the telegraph, developed an International Morse Code for moving forward communication. This code proved invaluable to the world during the wars to come. The US & Britain soon joined with Spain, abolished slavery, and set out to free slaves found on slave ships. The Opium War was going on between China, France, and Britain looking to snare society into a permanent stupor. While the Potato Chip was invented in Saratoga Springs NY, Ireland was experiencing a potato famine. International trade increased five times than in previous years. These faster ships now carried bacteria from port to port. Karl Marx's, "The Communist Manifesto" was published during this time and was used for promoting socialism and communism while trying to destroy all capitalism and the middle class. Meanwhile, in Pennsylvania, the first oil well was successfully drilled resulting in replacing whale oil with a new kind of liquid gold. A young, devout Baptist entered the oil refining business. His name was John Davidson Rockefeller. He was born near Ithaca NY in a small town that currently has under twelve hundred residents. John Rockefeller's father was a liar and a snake oil salesman that left his family penniless while escaping criminal charges. Despite his father, John Rockefeller is considered the wealthiest American of all time. During this time in history, the Gold Rush was in full swing in California and Australia.

Ascanio Sobrero was a university student who was scared by an accidental explosion while conducting experiments. The material he was using was considered too dangerous to be of any practical use and was impossible to handle. This opened the door for a fellow student, Alfred Nobel. His family business was suffering, and he found a way to salvage it. Nitroglycerin. His family began producing and selling this explosive substance. Sadly, he lost his younger brother in an explosion at his father's factory that was caused by this volatile substance. Nobel wanted to discover a safer method of handling Nitroglycerin and began experimenting more with it. Nobel eventually discovered a way to combine nitroglycerin with other compounds while wrapping it up for safer handling. He then patented this idea. Dynamite, and it resulted in tremendous wealth for his family.

Twenty years later Nobel wrote to a colleague about being prescribed a remedy for his chest pains. He said, "Isn't it the irony of fate that I have been prescribed Nitroglycerin to be taken internally! Trinitrin. They call it Trinitin, so as not to scare the chemist and the public." He refused to take the Nitroglycerin. It would be eighty years later before scientists would understand how nitroglycerin saved so many lives from potential heart attacks. Nobel died a few months later. Maybe Nobel could not understand how this explosive substance, when heavily diluted and taken internally, could have saved his life.

At this time in history, medicine was facing many uphill challenges. Science was slow to accept new technologies and applications. Germs were not fully understood, and practices were not in place to prevent the spread of disease or infection. Some believed these germs could not affect them because of their social status. John Snow discovered that a Cholera outbreak was a bacteria carried in food and water. He found it on the handle of a community water-well. He removed the handle and the outbreak ended. He couldn't explain "how" only the "what."

This timeframe gave birth to what is known today as the "Semmelweis Effect." This is a metaphor for the reflex-like tendency to reject new evidence or new knowledge because it contradicts established social norms, beliefs, or paradigms. With all the technology and new inventions, society continued to reject new evidence, because it conflicted with their beliefs. This rejection reflex is the Semmelweis Effect.

Dr. Ignaz Semmelweis was a Hungarian doctor practicing medicine at the General Hospital in Vienna, Austria. It had two maternity wards. One was staffed by midwives while the other by doctors and medical students. Today, we don't think twice about choosing a hospital with educated doctors to deliver babies. During this time, the doctor's ward was the last choice for those giving birth. Why? Puerperal Fever. This disease, also known as "childbed fever", caused the death of many new mothers. The chance of contracting Puerperal Fever was five times more likely to be contracted in the doctor's ward than in the midwife ward. It would strike fear in many expectant mothers who would sometimes rather take their chances of giving birth at home rather than the hospital. Dr. Semmelweis was perplexed and determined to solve this conundrum. His superiors at the hospital believed the disease was spread because of poor air quality. They implored him to give up on this mission, but he refused to give up. He studied the different practices and techniques of the midwives versus the doctors to find any discrepancies that could explain why these two hospital wards were so different. In his search to find the answer, he tested and ruled out different factors. Could it be the different birth positions? Could it be the stress on mothers? Could it be the noise made by the clergy during birthing?

Dr. Semmelweis was puzzled. That was until his friend and colleague contracted symptoms like Puerperal Fever after performing an autopsy on a woman who died from the disease. This turned his research in a new direction. Examining what happened during the autopsy, he discovered that his colleague cut his finger. He hypothesized that the cadaver was the missing piece in this puzzle. After taking a closer look at the procedures of the doctors, he discovered that many of them would perform autopsies before going directly to birth newborns. He also noticed that they didn't wash their hands or any instruments in between procedures.

During this time, many medical professionals believed that disease could be transferred through smell. He instructed the doctors to wash their hands and instruments with a chlorine solution to get rid of the smell. Dr. Semmelweis was unknowingly killing germs.

This reduced the deaths of puerperal fever to an amazing one percent. For the first time, the death rate was lower than that in the midwife ward. Unfortunately, this handwashing practice didn't stick. Despite the favorable results and many lives saved, the established medical field would not accept that they had dirty hands that had germs and caused this problem.

This era of so-called "gentlemen" was filled with pride. To question the status quo was looked down upon significantly. Men thought that based on their knowledge, social position, or genealogy, they were better than others. The very air they breathed was filled with a stench of self-righteousness. They were the cause of the deaths but wouldn't hear it.

The notion of germs was not yet understood. Dr. Semmelweis could not explain his findings scientifically. Furthermore, these medical doctors were gentlemen who believed they were superiorly fashioned and had impeccably clean hands that could not be contaminated.

Dr. Semmelweis confounded the issue by demonizing those doctors as murderers with contaminated hands responsible for the deaths of many. This did not go over well. Hundreds of lives were saved by implementing his methods of simply washing hands and instruments in chlorine. His theory was outright rejected. The established community that took offense to his claims wanted his voice quieted for good. They conspired with his wife to have him admitted into an insane asylum under false allegations. It didn't end well for Dr. Semmelweis. He died two weeks later.

Ten years later, Louis Pasteur scientifically explained the

impact of germs and pasteurization. In hindsight, the "Semmelweis Effect" was reborn. Dr. Semmelweis became known as "the savior of women" for his discovery of hand sanitation.

Pride can blind and deafen someone from seeing the actual truth. Truth is still there, even if it's not believed to be there or in Dr. Semmelweis' case ignored.

It's heartbreaking to imagine how many lives were lost to infection because of the pride of many "gentlemen" physicians. Their minds were so inflated by their ego. They were blinded and deafened by pride. They believed the lie.

Lies Mixed with Pride Blinds You.

Our lies, deceit, and blindness will hurt others. They will cause us to act irrationally. They force us to take positions in bias because we believe that we cannot be wrong. Today, many men reject what is true, especially when they don't understand the truth. They would rather believe the perceived comforts of a lie even if it hurts themselves or those close to them.

If ignorance is bliss, then maybe having blind knowledge is too. Knowledge does not automatically equal the acceptance of what is true and therefore, it may still leave you blinded from seeing the truth. You can be a very intelligent liar. Some of the most intelligent people on earth have rejected truth and believed lies. Knowledge does not by itself lead us to truth or honesty.

Educating a criminal to become more knowledgeable will just

make him a more knowledgeable criminal. Knowledge will not make a liar more truthful. People need more than knowledge to change into a person that's truthful. To be a person of truth is not a mind test. It does not matter how much you know. It's not even a test of will. What you decide doesn't change what is true. True change comes when you change internally. It's a heart test.

When you believe a lie to protect your ego, you are blinded from seeing the truth. It shrouds your heart from reality. You may think you know what is true, but everything you do is clouded by the limited visibility of your lies. Lies will cloud your eyesight and your judgment. If men continue to follow this path, it will ultimately lead to total blindness and despair.

There is still hope if we reach past these lies and grab hold of the truth. Are you willing to pay the price and let go of your past? Are you willing to expose the lies and admit the truth? Internal change will bring you into truth. Someone who is honest and cares for others. A man of integrity that is not consumed with himself but is watching over those he loves. A man not afraid to embrace a spiritual life and to change.

He Can Be Super Strong

A man's physical strength makes him feel rough, tough, and strong. It often feels like weakness to him when he looks beyond his physical strength and embraces inward change. Accepting this perceived weakness as his true strength is where he begins to develop the qualities of a truly powerful man.

Humility is not weakness. It is strength. It allows a man to see clearly and to hear vividly. It helps him to see the bigger picture in life. On the other hand, his ego would have stood in his way, making him unable to hear well or see clearly. Humility is his power to help others, rather than stepping over them. It slows him down just enough, so that he does not miss the opportunities presented all around him. Humility lifts others. In general, humility is a modest view of oneself. It means to go low. Going low does not mean to retaliate, or an eye for an eye. A humble man puts himself lower in the estimation of himself so others around him are seen by him as higher or of equal worth. In his mind, he lifts them and thinks of ways to help them improve. He takes actions that are in the best interest of others and not his own. With a modest view of himself, it allows him to raise his estimation of others for who they are. He truly values them. He treasures them. When a man is humble or is "low," he finds himself looking up, not down. A humble man does not look down on others but looks up at how high he can lift them. He uses his strengths to lift others to everything they should and could be. A humble man does not have to struggle to compete. He wins when others win. Humility is taking the focus off yourself and placing it on helping others.

Who would not like this? It's like having someone in your corner and someone who is always watching your back. They are like a trainer and a life coach free of charge. It's your lawyer that does not charge you for every minute. An accountant that adds to your bottom line. They are there to make you better.

Humility is only one characteristic of a real man. This humble man does not judge others based on their education, intellect, financial status, race, victories, or defeats. He sees them for who they are. He sees the way their thoughts, beliefs, and emotions will lead to productive or nonproductive behaviors. The humble man looks for the truth and is there to assist. He is someone who is not blinded by his own lies. His own life models what he looks for. He knows this and is a gracious recipient of all that is offered to him through humility. Humility is not a weakness. It's his super strength. It empowers him to be true and authentic. A humble man uses his ability to empower others. He raises them higher than they could ever go alone.

More than twenty-five thousand people each year attempt to climb Mount Kilimanjaro in Tanzania, Africa. It is the highest free-standing mountain in the world. The trek to the summit is rigorous. Climbers experience many different challenges along the way and some climbers never make it to the summit. Guides go through tremendous effort to get people ready for this climb of a lifetime. He packs gear, food, and emergency equipment for him and his team. He's made this climb hundreds of times, but he knows that no matter how much knowledge he has or how much he prepares, the mountain is always unpredictable.

To make it to the summit, the guide knows it will take more than a willingness and a desire to climb 19,341 feet. It will take more than just knowledge of the mountain to make this trek. Skill is paramount but alone won't allow for a successful mission. Humility allows the guide and his team to push aside their pride, ego, and previous successful climbs. This allows them to be alert, aware, and to prepare for the challenges that may come at them. The guide does not have time to play ego games when his and other climbers' lives are on the line. Confidence is different from ego. He knows his strengths and weaknesses.

He knows his climbers' weaknesses too. Together this will be a successful expedition.

Humility training makes us fit for life by helping mankind gain the endurance they need to succeed. It intertwines with our other positive skills making us balanced. With humility, we will have a balanced success climbing the mountains we face in life. Humility embraces the strength in others while recognizing their true value. This allows him to be stronger than he could ever be alone. It shifts a man's focus off himself and onto who we are together. Humble men are not consumed with themselves. They are willing to be what others need them to be. Men of true strength. True men are humble. Humble men don't need to be first, but value getting to their destination in life together.

King of The Hill

Some believe that man was made from dirt, from clay, and from the "dust of the earth". If this is true, then perhaps it makes him moldable. Maybe possessing the ability to adapt and change. He may need some guidance, some mentoring, and some training, but he can change.

He will eventually fall off that ivory throne of pride as he surrenders to humility each day. There is room for only one throne. If it's empty, he will take it. If you jump on it, he will fight you for it. He wants to be king of the hill. Men love to be king and to rule alone on the throne, but there is another way.

He can surrender that throne to God and take the place of being equal with other human beings. He should be a partner not a dictator. Only then will he not be in a place that is looking down upon women. He won't be looking down at others either. He will see others face-to-face, equal in value, and equal in worth. This is where men should be. A partner, not in a fight to be king of the hill or in a battle to be king or queen.

Growing up in cold New York State, where winters lasted six months of the year, there was a game we played called King of The Hill. After a heavy snowfall, piles of snow would appear everywhere as plow trucks worked endlessly clearing roads and parking lots. These parking lots would have the best snow mountains. Some of them were nearing 40 feet high. We couldn't wait to climb that mountain. The object of this game was to be the first one to the top of the hill. To be the only person left controlling the highest point. To be King of the Hill. This was not easy because with every step, the snow often shifted underneath you. Once at the top, you did everything possible to be the only one there by pushing everyone else down that was trying to dethrone you. By being the only one left on the top of this mountain of snow, you were named "King of The Hill". Many men are still fighting to be the king of the hill in their life. It is a fight that has casualties.

Men have been trying for years to remain king of the hill. They cannot live a lie and try to be king. The only way he will give up the struggle for being on the throne is through surrendering to God. He can't dethrone the one who should be there. God alone should be the only king in life leaving man in a place of equality with others.

Men must let go of their pride by giving up the lie, believing that they must always be in control. They must see past their arrogant thinking that they must always be the one in charge. Only then will he find his true self and become an honest man. One that has found his super strength. Humility! He will no longer be consumed with taking ultimate authority in his relationships. Living on an equal level with everyone else, he will see women for who they really are. A true partner in life and his equal.

A loving, honest, and humble man that is supportive of women being the best version of themselves. He is not in any way dismissive of your gifts, your strengths, your talents, or your value.

It's time for men to put away their pride and embrace true manhood. It is time to put on the strengths and qualities that define real men. Humility, mixed with honesty, will make you a real man. A man that the world will embrace and love to be around. A man that makes life better for everyone. A man that people always want to be with and be like. This is a true man, not living a lie.

So, if men are prepared to change, there is still hope. If he is willing to dethrone himself then watch out. He may surprise those around him so much that you won't be able to imagine life without him. If he has given up this game of "king of the hill" in life and has embraced women as his equal, then things are about to dramatically improve.

In his humility, he loses the need to only benefit himself. He knows that the more he helps women and others succeed in life, it will automatically benefit him too. He will rise equally as he encourages them. As he helps others climb to be the best version of themselves as possible, then he is there also being the best version of himself. A humble, super strong, successful man, and not a liar.

Questions for Self-Reflection

Do you see yourself as one who is proud in any area of your life?

How has pride blinded you from seeing clearly? Now ask someone else to answer this for you.

How has overestimating your own ability/strength put you in a vulnerable position?

How do you view humility?

How can being humble benefit those you love?

3

Stepping Over Others

I'm one to advocate for taking personal responsibility and not passing the blame on others or on society. In part, I must admit that our culture has added to the problem of selfishness. Is it wrong to want to be the winner or to always be first at everything at any cost? Many people may excel in getting to first place without lying their way to get to the top. The difference is in the journey they take or on the path they use to get there. Is that roadway paved with honest effort? Is it paved with lies? Are there remains of people you had to step over to get there? What would motivate someone to be like this? Why would someone step over others just to get ahead? Why would a man lie just to be "numero uno?" Why would you want to be King of The Hill at all costs?

Selfishness is sometimes hidden. It is sometimes obvious. It has motives that in some situations, could take years to expose. It has a secret mission. Its victims lay helpless after discovering

32

the truth that had been concealed for decades. They were never important at all to an extremely selfish person. What is selfishness anyway? Why do men feel the need to be so selfish? We need to be selfish to live our lives to some degree while providing a safe place to live and having food to eat. There is quite a difference between self-preservation and selfishness. Sometimes men simply get the meaning twisted. Self-preservation is the effort and work we do to survive. It exists in the world and society. We act in our self-interest to protect ourselves and our families. This self-preservation is something we all need.

It is more common and natural to see selfishness appear in some people who have yet to find their purpose in life. In their immaturity, they hold onto what they think they want while missing what they need. They have not taken the time to form deep relationships. This is where they find true value. Instead, they continuously take from the shallow relationships they have, instead of learning to protect, nurture, and deepen them. Being closed away, you are hiding in your cocoon of selfishness.

You don't have to give in to being selfish. This is done by thinking beyond yourself, your needs, and your wants. Search beyond yourself. Discover your dreams and your purpose. Include others in your future. Many young people have yet to figure out their true purpose in life. Without meaningful relationships, it creates an atmosphere where their time is spent taking care of only themselves. If you're single, maybe you can get away with being concerned for only yourself. It's a lonely way to live long-term. It won't score you any points if you're ever thinking of getting into a serious relationship. When you live this way, you're limiting who and what you can be.

Young people are not the only ones who are plagued by

selfishness. Those who refuse to grow up often remain selfish even though they may have many celebrated birthdays behind them.

Men, who have been stunted by certain hardships in life, may choose to continue to be selfish. They shut themselves off from others as a type of reflex to life's pain. They do this rather than learning to turn their pain into something gained.

Selfishness that goes unchecked and protected by lies will undermine the very fabric of trust that relationships are built on. Relationships are the network of life that brings fulfillment and companionship. This can come from friends, coworkers, and family members. Relationships that are destabilized through selfish behavior will lead you down a solitary path. It will eventually lead to a place of isolation. Relationships work best when there is an equal amount of giving and taking, but a selfish person knows only how to take. People create a sense of value from others knowing you have something to offer them. Selfish people operate in relational debt. Pretty soon that debt must be collected. The selfish man refuses to pay up and only digs his hole deeper.

Often the path to pleasure and profit can be exhilarating; sometimes making these selfish behaviors attractive. Selfish people will do whatever it takes. Even if their lies are hurting the people they care for and love.

Selfishness can be catchy, like a cold or a virus. It does not take long. Being around a selfish person will begin to influence you. There are a couple of ways you may respond in this type of situation. You may embrace it and catch selfishness. When you get bitten by the selfish bug you live for yourself. After all, it feels good to get what you want, when you want it. The intoxicating feeling of selfishness can be addictive. Once infected, it spreads fast and leaves you wanting more. It impacts your entire life. Your focus is just pleasing yourself. Now it's too late because you're a carrier. You are spreading selfish germs wherever you go. You cause others to choose to put up with your selfishness or become infected. It is a very volatile and toxic way to live. Consumed by selfishness. Another way you may respond, is to get as far away from that selfish person as you possibly can. Stay away to keep yourself from getting infected. Emotionally, you can only take so much of someone's selfish behaviors and lies until you're exhausted. It's wearisome and draining to keep up with their lies and all the activities centered around them. It takes a toll. You have nothing left to give. They have drained you of everything.

Selfishness is like driving a car on a racetrack. You are going one-way in a complete circle with no way out. This can drive you crazy until you finally realize you are going nowhere. This is not a relationship. This is a claustrophobic trap. It leaves those within it, with an increasing desire to get out.

What happens when you are in a relationship with a selfish person? They always want to be first and are unpredictable. Just as if they were driving down a busy highway, they swerve and speed, turn in front of you, and drive dangerously. They disobey traffic laws. In relationships, they make choices that benefit only themselves. They lie and cheat to get what they want. They have no rules. Their haphazard driving puts others at risk of an accident. Unfortunately, you are now on the side of the road and in a ditch. You trusted someone to obey the "relational traffic law", but they didn't. They disrespected you and betrayed your trust. They wanted to be first at any cost, even if that cost was causing you pain.

The price paid by selfishness and lies is immediately collected from others. Even though the liar may not even know it. Payment is later demanded from them. Often, it's paid by those closest to them or even children who are trapped in their circle of selfishness.

Healthy relationships balance giving and taking. It is like dancing. There is leading, following, giving, and taking. You move in a way to not step on each other's toes. Movements, while working together, create a beautiful display of grace and skill. Try dancing with someone who wants to do things their way and is selfish. This causes pain, not security. They are comfortable being the only one on the dance floor. The evidence is by how they step all over you and cause a scene. It's not a pretty picture or pleasant to watch. It causes your dance partner to feel uncomfortable and to feel cornered. They just want it to stop and can't wait for it to be over. Healthy relationships create a feeling of security and comfort. They are two people working together feeling loved in the dance of life.

Selfishness harms those around you, and generally just hurts. The longer lies mask selfish agendas and go unexposed, the more they hurt those caught in their extensively built web of lies.

Selfishness can be seen everywhere. Here are some examples:

- Politicians use their platform of public service for personal gain. They are always smiling for the camera while forgetting those who helped them get where they are with their votes. They do not remember that they are public servants. Instead, they hurt their constituents through selfishness. They have stepped on others to get where they want to be, the spotlight. While in office, they obtain substantial wealth. They have forgotten who they represent. They have not forgotten themselves. After all, they come first.

- The minister who uses their influence from the pulpit to build an empire. They are betraying the trust of those who gave their time, energy, and money. Congregants who wanted to help the community through their church, discovered that their leaders had another vision. Their own gain and a hidden agenda. They were primarily working on building their own kingdom, not God's kingdom.

- The university professor who was supposed to inspire unity in diversity, but now is determined to reproduce their own opinion in students. This limits the growth of their students from developing the ability to challenge societal norms that make us better people and the world a better place. They have traded away a good education for cloning their own selfish thinking.

- The news reporter who gave up on truth and fact-checking just to attract a higher social media attention and more followers. This leaves their communities to find out for themselves what story is true, and which is false. All because the public can't trust the journalist's research anymore. News is just a story that resembles a fairytale.

- The professional athlete whose selfish behavior is setting a bad example for thousands of young people to follow. They don't care, they just do what they want. They live how they want with no regard for those looking up to them.

- The actor who lives in a Hollywood bubble and has become a professional lecturer. They lack any common ground with others in our society to offer an opinion of value. They have allowed themselves to be publicly exploited for wealth while pretending it is normal behavior for everyone. They think they are normal and can relate to everyone, when they are not, and can't.
- The Lawyer whose entire practice pivots on who can lie the best. There is no desire for the truth or what "actually" has happened. Their only desire is to get others to believe their lies, so it looks true.

If these platforms of influence and others are used to hide selfish motives, they will not only destroy the destiny of those who trust them, but they will tarnish an entire generation with their lies and their selfishness. These men and women tend to focus on themselves. Their every action and choice in life is for their own pleasure. They do not care about those that get hurt in the process. Selfish people don't consider the children that happen to be in their way. They don't care about adults either. They see others "as a means to an end," their personal satisfaction. These selfish liars are destroying our society. They step over others only to get what they want. They are building a kingdom to themselves.

Political Turmoil

We are living in a time of a politically diverse and polarized environment. The very word "politician" seems to be synonymous with the word "liar". This makes us feel powerless to do anything about it because that is the way it has always been. Some have given up on politicians telling us the truth and we seem to be alright with lies. Does it matter which political party you stand with if lies continue to be mistaken as truth?

Lobbyists represent all different points of view to Congress. No matter what the lobbyists are representing, they want their voice heard. But who do they believe? How do they know what is true? It seems that finding out the truth in Washington has been replaced by rubber-stamping the best bill that fits political motives. Has truth been cast out of the House and Senate? If yes, it's because the American people have departed from "truth" themselves. Since "We the People" have allowed ourselves to believe lies, it makes it easier for politicians to please us with our low expectations of truth, honesty, and integrity. Are we believing a lie as truth? Whether we are conscious of it or not, we will have negative results from lies.

It is obvious that this is a large issue and mainly a leadership problem. Political leaders have wielded their influence over the masses like a magic wand, using their trickery against us to gain trust. Who else are we going to believe if not our leaders? Don't they represent us? Oh, how far the mighty politicians have fallen. To blame the American people alone would be naive. We may have allowed this but they are doing this.

Look up a definition of a politician and you will find that it is a person who acts in a manipulative and devious way to gain advancement within an organization. Who would hire anyone like this if it was listed on their resume? No one. What if their campaign slogan was, "I will deceptively get my way at your expense." This is exactly what we are seeing in today's political climate. They mask the words they say to appeal to their party line and constituents that gave them their vote. The difference is it is all a lie.

Politicians have gone from public servants to public officials. Public servants are elected individuals who represent the people they serve with an understanding of their role and responsibility. They have dropped the word servant and forget those they were meant to serve. Instead, they serve themselves. They should follow the example of the Rotarian motto, "Service Over Self". Today, politicians have changed into something different and have this backwards. Their role as an elected official has transformed from a serving function to a governing function. This highlights their position more than their duty to the job they were elected to do. Where did the honor and integrity go? Where is the accountability to make sure elected officials are acting responsibly for those they were meant to serve? As our expectations for politicians continue to get lower and lower, the level of integrity will also continue to decrease as selfishness and lying continue to go unchecked. Their new motto seems to be "Me over You." It seems that we now serve them.

In America, we assume that when someone won a political position, they rolled up their sleeves and got to work for everyone. Yes, we still fought our views and stood on our political grounds. Whoever won at the end of the day was the elected official for everyone, even if they didn't vote for them. Today, things are quite different. When a politician wins office, it is assumed they will advance their political position as far as they can regardless of its impact on those within their jurisdiction. Time in the office is their time to divide. Division and disrespect are commonplace. Lies are everywhere. People are mad and confused. Selfishness, greed, and control have consumed politicians in office. In America, it looks like we have lost our way. Where is the honor and respect for the office that we have entrusted to them?

We no longer want what is good for our country or our people. Instead, we only want what is good for ourselves. The famous words of President John F. Kennedy, "Ask not what your country can do for you, ask what you can do for your country," has changed. All we hear now from others and politicians is, "What can be done for me?"

We need our politicians to see things differently and be different. Consider this a call to truth. Lies that are now expected have ruined our country. One way for things to change is for our world's leaders to change. It is time to put all people first regardless of their political position. Value people for who they are. Are not all people created equal? It is time to serve people again and resist acts of selfishness. It is time to commit to serving a higher agenda. Serve us all! Be known for integrity and honesty, even if in your honesty you lose a few votes. Become true public servants again.

You have heard it said, "Put your money where your mouth is." In other words, be willing to pay for your opinions and your beliefs. Back up what you say! Politicians need to mean what they say and say what they mean. What about when their opinions and beliefs are harmfully selfish? We won't be able to pay that price. It's way too high! The payment to back up your selfishness will cost us our souls and our freedoms. Instead, let us put our hearts where our mouth is. Pay the price inwardly! Love your neighbor as yourself. Redefine current expectations. Change the very definition of who and what you are. Serve again. Make us proud you were elected. All of us. Not just those who voted for you. Serve us all, not yourself. Be selfless and truthful.

Let your time in the office be earmarked, remembered, and honored by the generations to come. Let us not remember you by how you fattened your wallet, increased your political agenda, or became more popular. Politicians, please be known for how you unselfishly reached across party lines and unified our country. How you used your voice to make known the real needs of those we often can't hear. Let us remember how you enriched our lives with policies that made us better. Let us remember you for serving us selflessly.

Spiritual Devastation & Disappointment

Those who are given the most trust often are the ones in positions to disappoint us the most. The mother whom you thought loved you more than anything in the world but later you find out she loved her drugs or bottle more. This can be devastating. The father, meant to protect you from harm but is so caught up in his own world that he does not see the pain inflicted on you from others. His neglect could leave you wounded.

In addition to trusting one's own family, a great deal of trust has been put into trusting spiritual leaders. People place their deep trust in ministers, pastors, or priests who are called to serve in a higher capacity than the rest of us. Some ministers, who are supposed to help you find your meaning and purpose in life, instead selfishly destroy your hope and future. They betrayed the very trust you committed to them. We are living in a world where ministers, pastors, and priests are engaging in acts of blatant, immoral selfishness. How can this be happening? They are violating people's trust, misusing men and women, and committing actions against children. This is unthinkable. Some ministers think they are working "for" God, instead of working "with" God. "For" is the label they use to do what they want to do while living a double life. A double standard. Telling people one thing while doing the opposite themselves. Many of them would not want their parishioners or the public to know what they are doing. They are not partnering with God but using people for selfish gratification. When finally exposed, some of them want to escape their problems and leave their life behind. This can create the ultimate act of selfishness. Suicide. Leaving a mess for everyone left behind to clean up. If they were working "with" God, they would be a partner with God in everything they do.

Suicidal thoughts are something that should be taken seriously. We must sympathize with those who struggle with this issue. This has a mental health side along with a spiritual side. The spiritual side is a battle between forces trying to get you to give up. End it all. Evil may sometimes whisper but a minister should be someone who doesn't listen or dwell on those evil thoughts. Ministers should know how to win this mental battle. They have been previously tested and must pass this test beforehand. Others are counting on them. The mental health side of this ideation is totally different. The person suffering from this dwells on these negative thoughts without resistance. Mental health issues can also be caused chemically. A minister suffering mental health issues is in the wrong profession. They may cause more harm than good. There are many ways to continue doing work for God that is not full-time shepherding people. Just like a surgeon who has trembling hands, he needs to consider other options. This is just like the person who is in ministry with mental health issues. I'm not suggesting that someone who is struggling with mental health issues can't help others. I am, however, suggesting that a lead minister over hundreds of people is not the place for this to be on display. A selfish person will hold on to that position of power even at the cost of hurting others.

To make matters worse, how do all these problems with ministers get covered up? What organization protects this kind of behavior? A selfish one. Not a Godly one. The very principles in which these organizations are founded are violated by hideous actions. They are just covered up like they never happened. These men who did this are like counterfeit artwork propped up in an art gallery pretending to be authentic. They are liars with lies from the top to the bottom. Hidden lies. Instead of exposing the lies and the crimes committed in their organization, these institutions just make it worse. Causing insult to injury. Those in authority who were meant to hold these perpetrators accountable, have made them untouchable. They didn't protect those who were hurt. These were the very people they vowed to help. These organizations are not helping the people they were meant to serve, but only protecting those who have sworn allegiance to them. They are like a religious mafia whose mission is to please the godfather instead of God the Father. Positioned in wealth and status, they have morphed into the very evil they set out to defeat. In this massive cover-up, ministers who have committed these crimes have become a lie. They are reproducing lies to protect their ego. They betray their own people and themselves. They step over people to meet their own selfish needs. They create utter chaos and confusion. This undermines the very center of security within our society, the family.

Selfishness can find its way easily into the hearts and lives of liars. Any form of selfishness can take a minister away from their primary purpose of serving God and their congregants. The word minister means to serve. God has given them to help people rather than to hurt them. A minister is like a good waiter that you hardly know is there. They listen skillfully to your order, always remain polite, and anticipate your needs before you even ask. Good pastors set examples to serve in ways that benefit you the most. They fill you with spiritual food that's presented in a way that is healthy for you to grow. There is a cooking show where a famous chef helps fix failing restaurants. One thing I have observed in many of these restaurants is how horrifically disgusting the kitchen is. Often, this famous chef would stop everything just to make everyone clean the kitchen.

The kitchen is where all the food preparation takes place in a restaurant. You expect it to be clean, organized, and well-managed. A pastor's private life and home are like his kitchen. It's the place where everything is prepared, including their sermon. I often wonder what a pastors' so-called "kitchen" looks like based on the messages they prepare. This may be a good time to clean up your private life. This is the hidden place that no one sees but God.

If you are a minister, remember you are called to serve God and the community, not yourself. You were sent to build God's kingdom, not your kingdom. You were meant to set the example, not to be a bad example. You are intended to live with character, not be a character. You are called to love and not hate. You are supposed to be the best of us while living as the least of us. You may seem foolish in the eyes of our culture, but you are not fools. You are living like a foreigner, not a king or a pauper either, but somewhere in between.

You serve in a way that does not make you rich but makes you the recipient of much appreciation while making others abundant in truth. You love others when they agree with you and when they don't. You are often the voice of absolute reason and truth.

Ministers should be deserving of the trust that we have bestowed on them. We trust them to live Godly. This example will always be remembered. Good pastors make the necessary sacrifices to help others accomplish their dreams instead of using others to selfishly accomplish their agendas. I do believe in forgiveness, even for fallen selfish ministers. I don't think that in every situation forgiveness means restoration. When you selfishly hurt others, you break their trust. Trust takes time to heal. It's not all about you!

The College Collapse

Today, selfishness can be seen everywhere, including in our universities. The very basis on which they were founded, many with pure intentions, has transformed into something completely different. This can be clearly seen in how these institutions no longer reflect the mottos they were founded on. What is a motto anyway? It's a phrase that guides the principles or beliefs of an organization or an institution. It's interesting how far many colleges have moved away from their motto. Their original message. If you were to visit or attend many of these campuses today and compare their original motto to their current teaching, you may have a good case for false advertising. What was once believed, is no longer. It is a lie. Can you imagine that Ivy League colleges like Harvard, Yale, and Princeton, once had mottos that said, "For the Glory of Christ," "Truth for Christ and the Church," "Truth," "Pure Light and Truth," and "Under the Protection of God She Flourishes?" I wonder what motto many of these universities should hold today. Maybe some of these mottos should be changed to reflect their current image as said, "For the Glory of Man", "Lies for Our Culture", "Pure Shadows and Lies", and "Under the Motive of Lying She Hides".

We would expect, to a small degree, institutions of learning to evolve if they are a true university. Things have changed a lot. University means "Unity in Diversity." There was a time when the thought of learning was that we can agree to disagree. That has changed in today's culture. Today, many believe that if you don't agree with me, I can't listen to you or respect you. This is a false assumption. Perhaps I could blame the colleges themselves. Watch what happens when you try to disagree with the professor in many of the current college climates. It seems that dialogue and inquiry can only be done if it's in agreement with the status quo or current establishment. The professor is like a demigod. Living in his ideological bubble and lecturing the world from his podium. He is expecting us to agree without question. Violate his opinion and there will be a repercussion to your decent. Why has learning at university become indoctrination rather than open learning and rational discussion? The professor has positioned himself to reproduce men and women as a clone of his own thoughts and ideas. This is the ultimate selfish behavior. He lives only to replicate himself. Professors are determined to clone people's minds to think and believe as they do. This does not create a world of free thinkers. It creates a mass army of individuals who think like him and creates a society who believe only they are right. What if they are believing a lie? What if they are wrong in their philosophy or belief? This assumption is not even considered. We are playing "Russian Roulette" with our young people's minds and beliefs. Have you tried having a discussion with a college graduate? In your conversation, it does not take long to realize they think they know everything. Some of this behavior is, of course, their age and their excitement and energy. Almost as if they have the same beliefs as their professors do. They think they can't possibly be inaccurate. This is what they have been told. They argue with anyone that implies they are wrong. Why should they believe anything less? Why would they be lied to by their instructors?

Many professors have set students up with selfish lies. There is a price to pay for teaching and believing those lies. These professors selfishly promote their own political and social agendas, rather than promoting the individual growth of students. Instead of creating a foundation for them to build their own beliefs, they use students as a platform to walk out their agendas. It may take years, but eventually these disillusioned young adults will come face to face with life. When life's pain and troubles happen, the truth will prevail. It often takes pain to help us realize what we believe.

The ultimate selfishness of a college institution is not that they sold their students sweatshirts covered in their logo and colors, but they sold them lies that they still believe years later.

Did your college allow free discussion? Congratulations! They are not producing robots but real-thinking, world changers.

It's time we put the truth back into the classroom. We need to make sure professors are not using students as a means for their personal agendas. Universities should not be using students' talents and strengths to accomplish what they want them to do. We, as a society, should get behind students and support their growth. We need to show them personally, who to be by setting an example.

Colleges, professors, and graduates should embrace truth and honesty. They must be willing to make the necessary sacrifices to be better for themselves and our society. We don't need liars and cheaters. We need truth back in classrooms!

Media Blunder

News is not anything new. For centuries people have been wanting to know what is going on around them, and for centuries it has been corrupted.

What is the news anyway? News means "what is new." Everyone is always interested in discovering what is new. This tremendous interest in "the new" has led many to realize that if they can control this information, they have power. A power to shape people's minds, thoughts, opinions, and beliefs. We all want to know what is going on in our neighborhood and around the world. Many have capitalized on this information.

Today news has evolved into something that is very opinionated rather than reporting what is "new." It started many years ago. Travelers would bring news to other places from far away. The townspeople would depend on the person traveling and delivering the news to relay the message correctly. Ancient cities had town criers that would walk around sharing what is new. The news. Later people would gather around the public square or market where edicts would be read to townspeople. Illiteracy was the norm. Those who couldn't read depended on those speaking, to tell the truth. Their reliability of news was truly at the mercy of the one speaking. An invention changed the way news was distributed, the printing press. It started replacing the town crier form of news. This forever changed how people relied on receiving news. Now people can read it for themselves and make their own judgments. That is if they could read. Literacy was no longer just for the nobility but was now a desire for the common man. It was a great motivator to learn to read. Newspapers became the "what's new" of the day. This continued until the radio was invented and started interrupting "regularly scheduled programming" to bring you "late-breaking news." Once again, news was spoken. Newspaper sales plummeted as people gathered around the radio. As a response to this, the newspaper started printing extra newspapers to get more readers just as news was breaking. "Extra! Extra! Read all about it!" The radio, during World War I, would have first-hand interviews with soldiers from the front. People at home heard reports about the war for the first time. The world seemed to get a little smaller. This continued until television became the hottest new news source. News stations began forming as television became popular. Now people can hear and see the news. Seeing the news added more assurance that you are hearing the truth. No longer just listening to what people are saying but watching them added a layer of trust to the news being reported. In 1960, the first presidential debate was televised, swaying voters by not only what was said but also by what was seen. Families would eventually gather every evening to listen to the six o'clock news. In time, reporters no longer saw the need to check all the facts. The next news story needed to be ready in hours not days. Opinions and discussions began to fill in the time needed for the twenty-four-hour news networks. News became entertainment. When computers hit the market, the internet changed the news world again. Now people can access information from around the world almost instantly. It is at this time news reporting evolved to keep up with the internet speed. Once again, we find ourselves, like centuries before, dependent on someone else for truthful news. The problem is that political news has always been communicated with bias throughout time. Truth has become hidden in the media today. Facts and opinions have been so mixed together, people do not know who to trust anymore. Lies have become common. Fact-checking is no longer the new normal. It's now a phrase you say to earn blind trust without any evidence. If we now watch the news, you have countless options. Even if every single station reported the same story, it would have a different twist or opinion. Even if they are discussing the same topic, the way they present it is completely different. It's all about them trying to get someone to believe it to be true the way they see it, even if it's not true at all. If they can get enough people to believe the story they are pitching, then it must be true.

Those who push their narrative only care about their ratings, numbers, popularity, and their secret hidden agenda. All this boils down to is, money, money, money, and power.

The extreme selfishness of these lies is so viciously apparent at times. It's mind-blowing! There is an agenda that is selfishly being pushed on society. They don't care about the impact that it has or who they hurt.

They have traded the American soul for cash and prostituted honor for fame. They have redefined the rules of engagement and changed the very meaning of truth and in their wake, devastation follows. Homes are flooded with lies and propaganda to twist our thinking.

Violence has erupted, spitting out hate, and lava is flowing out crime. Lives are burned to the ground leaving only ash. It's a tornado of lies trying to bury an entire generation and a tsunami that seems to be unstoppable.

When will it end? When will we stop listening to their deception?

The American people are sick of all the lies, they just want the facts, the truth. We can then take the facts and make up our own minds. Let us do with the news what we want to do, not what you want us to do. Let us decide how to think. Not how you want us to think.

We need our media to go back to the truth and become the investigators they were meant to be. We need them to check their sources and double-check the facts. Question motives behind each story.

We want to trust you again, but we need you to earn that right. Stop using your platform to take away our freedom and truth. Bring us the truth! Then maybe you can earn back our trust and sit at our tables again.

We need the media to go back in time and take lessons from the fictional radio character, Joe Friday. He was a detective known for solving crimes, sticking to the rule book, and the famous phrase, "Just the facts Ma'am, and nothing but the facts."

The same is true today. Just stick to the facts, nothing but the facts.

The First Amendment

"Freedom of speech" is the excuse that many people use to say whatever they want to say.

Just because you have the right to say something, does it

mean you have to say it? No, of course not. We choose to say what we want to say. When someone says something, which many times comes from hurt or rejection, we scream, "It's a free country! I can say what I want." People often say it is their first amendment right to say what they want to say but do they know what the first amendment says? Do they know its intent? The first amendment says, "Congress shall make no law respecting an establishment of religion or prohibiting the free exercise thereof; or abridging the freedom of speech, or of the press; or the right of the people peaceably to assemble, and to petition the government for a redress of grievances. The first amendment guarantees that there not be laws made that would make one religion a forced state religion. This was put in place because whatever the ruling monarchy believed became the religion everyone else had to follow. Our ancestors came to this country specifically for this freedom. Others were killed for their dissent from their political and religious views. Our founding fathers wanted to make sure that Congress would not make a law that prohibits you from exercising your religion freely. No law can be made to limit freedom of speech, or the press, or the right to assemble in peace. Freedom protects our right to speak and does not limit the right to say foolishly whatever we want to say. It also protects the assembling in peace but not if it is destructive. What is "freedom of speech"? It is the freedom to communicate verbally or in writing to others. It is not the freedom to do what we want. We have rights. We need to use these rights the right way. In a way that is beneficial, not harmful to our society. In 1919 a court ruling, Stench vs. The U.S. ruled that the freedom of speech, either written or spoken, is restricted if it presents a clear and present danger to society and if it would incite action that would harm others. The example given is someone who chooses to scream fire in a crowded room when there is no fire. The panic may potentially cause harm. It may be legal to say whatever you want to say, but it is not beneficial. For something to have benefit means that it is for good. Many people waste their freedom to spew hatred, lies, and angry rhetoric. Choose to use your freedom for good. The First Amendment protects many people to freely speak their opinions. There is a lie that has been believed that someone has a right, within this First Amendment, to do what they want to do. This amendment does not provide for freedom to destroy personal or public property, stop traffic, and cause people potential danger. Rioting in the streets is not our freedom, it is chaos. Violence is not protected by First Amendment rights. Believing that is a lie even if you think it is not.

Missing the Goal

We love sports in America: football, basketball, hockey, boxing, mixed martial arts, and more.

We don't all love how much athletes are paid. According to Forbes, the National Football League's (NFL) top ten paid players will earn 424 million dollars in combined salary, licensing, endorsements, and bonuses for that year. One National Basketball Association (NBA) player earned over thirty-four million dollars in 2018. The enthusiasm for sports in America and its impact on our society is proven by the amount of money spent on this entertainment. Whether these athletes want it or not, their status makes them automatically on a public stage. Their behaviors and actions are often an example of what our youth emulate. There are many adult super-fans as well. Many athletes do a great job of being role models. They don't separate who they are in their game time from the rest of their life. They are the same person on the field and off the field. They understand that what they do on the field and off the field is equally as important. Being watched continuously by fans, they should act accordingly with proper behavior. There is no "off" switch for being a famous athlete.

There is nothing more annoying than an extravagantly paid athlete acting like a two-year-old throwing a temper tantrum, selfishly wanting their own way. It's like a child with a multi-million-dollar bank account. Think about how your children would grow up if they could buy whatever they wanted without any guidance or budget. It would get out of control and in some ways outright dangerous.

Wisdom teaches us the necessity of understanding responsibility in life. Athletes should not waste precious time and resources. Character creates a protective bubble against destructive forces. What may be good, may not be good for us right now. What may be beneficial in limits, is lethal in certain quantities. Nitroglycerin in small doses is used to help those having chest pains while in large doses is used in dynamite.

Moderation and patience can save many lives from self-destruction. These qualities are developed, not purchased.

It's sad to see some of today's athletes void of true wealth. The kind that money can't buy. Many men go from childhood to adulthood without ever really growing up. They embrace selfish tendencies and behaviors that revolve around getting their own way. It's sad that many professional athletes don't allow life's challenges and hardships to help them become better, and more mature.

These men go through their teens and college years with blinders on in a protective cocoon-like environment. They generally don't have to deal with anything demanding. Hard life issues that require real character. They are good at a couple of things: hiding their man-child so that others can't see their immaturity and getting people to focus on their notable ability and performance. Rather than being a true man they are living a lie.

Athletes are some of life's so-called heroes who are idolized for their abilities and because they are wealthy. As long as they keep performing, fans put up with their tantrums, lack of manhood, childlike behaviors, and their messes. Who is left to clean it all up and who will hold them accountable? Someone must!

Our society is watching them. They want to be just like them. They want their fame, money, ability, lack of responsibility, and selfish attitude to do whatever they want to do.

There is hope. It's never too late for them to grow up and for men to turn into real men. Inwardly, there is the human innate capacity for change to occur quickly. They can be who they were meant to be. A person of mature character is waiting for them.

We can see this today in some of our professional athletes who either matured before they were famous or because of being famous. Their athleticism is not their greatest skill. They have been given the resources and the potential ability within themselves to be life's greatest men and women. They show the world what matters and reveal to us their true net worth, setting an example for all to follow. This makes true the saying to whom much is given much is required. They are our true heroes who are paid well for a talent that draws the attention of thousands. There are many athletes who go beyond themselves to help others in our society. They value others and help the less fortunate. They use their wealth for good not just for extravagant living. Through their selflessness, they pave the way to a bright future for us all. They should not waste their time with politics, media games, and divisive issues. They have too much value than to prostitute their true self-worth. Their highest internal value is to set an example. They can make the most difference outside of their athletic arena. When their time to perform has ended, their example won't. Their legacy will carry on. Of all the things that we will remember about them, we will remember more what they stood for and their character than what they were paid to do. Professional athletes have had to make many personal sacrifices for their careers. Athletic self-sacrifice is centered on making personal sacrifices for their personal benefit. Self-sacrifice is the sacrifice that is made for the benefit of others.

The Olympic Games displays more than mere ability, it reveals the depth of who each athlete is. It's on this world platform that true heroism is often displayed before our eyes. In the 2016 Olympics, the women's 5,000-meter race was underway in Rio de Janeiro, Brazil. With a determination for first place and to represent their country at their best, runners took off in a head-to-head competition. New Zealand's Nikki Hamblin, prepared for this moment her entire life. She tragically fell into American runner Abbey D'Agostino during the race. What happened next revealed why they both possessed much more than athletic ability. They helped each other up and continued arm in arm until they both finished the race. Winning no longer mattered, finishing did. No one remembers who finished the race first. We all know who won! This was an outstanding display of sportsmanship, character, and the human spirit. While others were given a medal of bronze, silver, and gold, these two runners displayed to the world the gold deep within their hearts. They impacted the world and set an example for everyone to follow. They pushed away selfishness at that moment and showed us the value of personal sacrifice to help others. They were given the prestigious International Fair Play Award for their outstanding conduct in the spirit of fair play. The lie was that they were sent by their country to win the race. The truth was that they won first place in many hearts all over the world.

Pierre de Coubertin the father of the modern-day Olympic Games said, "The important thing in life is not the triumph but the struggle, the essential thing is not to have conquered but to have fought well."

Self-Sacrifice

Self-sacrifice is the truth that is needed to overcome the lie of selfishness. It requires a change of mind, attitude, and making the right decisions. Allowing yourself to develop true character and to focus on others will take a lot of sacrifices. You may have to give up on some things or add some things. For example, when building character, you will have to give up selfish thinking and add some protective boundaries. Just like a building's integrity is only as good as its foundation, your character is only as good as your thoughts. You may discover cracks in your thinking that you have allowed to remain there for years. These noticeable cracks must be repaired. You will go right back to your old selfish way of thinking if they are not repaired. In keeping your selfish thinking and behaviors, you won't be able to support the growth and new construction that will help you to endure the weight of life's challenges. Changing these thoughts and behaviors will help you build taller and help the new you grow. You may have to do some digging. This may take some sacrifice and time. You can rebuild your foundation and become a better person.

For true change to occur you must turn around the way you think. You must change the way you act. Everything will change as your mindset changes. Changing into the "new you" will take sacrifice. Set boundaries for personal accountability. Protect what is important to you. This is the only way to maintain the new changes and new way of thinking.

What kind of sacrifices do you need to make? What boundaries need to be set? This depends on what you are building. If you want the new you to be more truthful, you must sacrifice by not lying and not always wanting your own way. Build trust with others through honesty. Be honest. You may have to admit you did something wrong. Be determined to be honest. Be trustworthy so that others can count on you to keep your word.

Do you want to be closer with your loved ones? This will require spending more time with them. The decisions you make with your time will show them what you truly value. You must set boundaries that will protect your time and increase the value you place on your relationships. You may have to sacrifice doing what you want to do. You may even have to surrender your alone time. But in doing this you will have more time to spend with your loved ones and continue to get to know them. During the 2020 coronavirus epidemic, families were forced to stay home. Schools were closed and people had to work remotely. Everyone was required to socially distance themselves from others. More time with family was now mandated. Many people had taken for granted the little time they had with loved ones. During this time at home, they were able to create memories that will last forever. Looking back, they will realize how they previously had missed many precious moments due to selfish behavior. Hopefully, going forward, they made the necessary changes to unselfishly build more lasting memories.

In helping men with relationships, they must realize this truth. True men are not slaves to pornography. They don't stare down women as they walk by. They respect and honor women. The boundaries you set, if you are to change, are to not allow yourself to disrespect women in thought or action. Every time you're tempted, you think of how much you appreciate, honor, and respect women. You don't view them as objects but someone's daughter, someone's sister, and someone's mother.

Change is more than just actions. It must carry over into your thinking and how you feel. You must push away the desire to be selfish and stop the lies that promote selfish behavior. Be willing to change by making the necessary sacrifices that are needed to destroy self-centeredness. Take back your relationships by building them on a new foundation, one that is not centered around yourself and your lies, but is built on sacrifice, honesty, and truth.

Be the man with a vision to build something great. Be willing to make the sacrifices necessary to build it well. It always amazes me how much effort men will put into lies. How much time they will put into trying to do something illegal. How about taking all that energy and focusing it on building something good? Why not create something true and honest that will bring others closer to you? This will make you a happier man. In the end, if you put in the effort and sacrifice, you will build a life of joy, satisfaction, and true contentment.

Questions for Self-Reflection

How important is it for you to be first or always number one?

How do you feel about being in second or third place?

How has selfishness been a part of your life?

Has your selfish behavior hurt those you care about?

What self-sacrifices can you make for those you love?

4

The Learning Curve

What is a lie? When does a little lie turn into a big lie? What is a little white lie? What makes them all so different?

Some people will sit down and plan their deceitful lies in detail. When you plan to lie on purpose, there is always someone who gets hurt by it. Lies violate trust. Lies distort reality. Lies bring confusion. Lies can destroy a community. They hurt relationships.

A lie can be with the intent to cause someone harm or on the other hand just to just get away with something. Either way, there is a price to pay for telling lies and someone always gets hurt in the process. People have created different categories of lying to minimize and rationalize certain behaviors to be acceptable.

There are generally only two types of lies. Within one of these two categories of lying there is a determining factor whether it's acceptable or not. Intent determines if it is "actually" a lie or not.

There is a lie of omission and a lie of commission. All lies fall within either of these two categories yet will vary in degree.

Lies of Commission

A lie of commission is a lie that you commit intentionally. Your motive was to keep someone from the truth on purpose. This is the worst of all lies because it often involves malicious intent. It is often premeditated. You know exactly what you are going to do. You planned and plotted. Much effort and time has gone into preparing your lie.

Lies of commission are justified by either over-generalizing or minimizing. When someone is over-generalizing, they will say something like, "Everyone does it". They are wrong! Because everyone does it, does not make something right or wrong. Overgeneralizing fails to take personal responsibility by blaming others, but not themselves.

The person minimizing will often say, "This is my decision. It's my choice. It's no big deal." They believe their lies will only impact themselves." Minimalizing fails to see the scope of impact that personal decisions and choices have on others. They can't see how their web of lies spin a wide, deep, and dark trap for others. It snares many all around them and often even them-selves. When one lie is spun, it makes it necessary to continue to spin others. This cycle continues until a lie is out of control or it is exposed. Once exposed, it begins to reveal the casualties of those hurt by it. The pain and consequence may or may not be enough to stop the liar from lying. Often the full impact of their lies remains hidden.

When caught in their lie, the person lying may or may not learn from their mistakes. If they do learn, they will grow and mature. If they don't, the cycle continues.

When given a choice, many young men choose the easy way out by lying to avoid negative consequences. This is instead of being truthful. If a young man chooses to continue down this path, with each lie he tells, the lines of truth become more blurred. Lines of truth keep people on course. Just like lines that are put on the roadway keep passengers in vehicles safe, truth protects our life. The white line on the edge of the road may not seem important during the daytime but at night the truth is that it keeps cars from going randomly off the road. A young man may think that hiding the truth is going to be beneficial, but then it leaves him in a ditch with no way to get out. Without taking the hard road of truth, he may never learn from those life experiences. Life throws us opportunities to grow and change, but the more difficult choice of being honest is a decision that lies within. Truth is not always the easiest decision, but it defends itself.

Men who depend on lying have blurred vision. It's like driving a car on a dark road when the windshield is all fogged up. It's a roadway you have never been on before. Your high beams are on, your fan is on high, wipers are in continual use, and you still can't see clearly. It makes driving conditions difficult, stressful, and potentially dangerous. Lying often makes a man unable to see the difference between what is true and what is false. Those who trust lies become someone who cannot be trusted. They can no longer see the long-term impact of their lies.

They may justify these lies by limiting the degree of responsibility for their choices, trying to shelter themselves from the consequences of their lies. They may dilute their guilt by comparing their actions to others'. Diluted guilt is still guilt.

In their immaturity, all they see are justifications. Their conscience over time becomes poisoned by lies. It is no longer effective for determining truth on its own. Their vision is marred and foggy. They have no clear direction anymore. They need more light. More truth. It's just like adding fog lights to a car. They help make the road clearer when it's dark and foggy. Truth also lights up your life.

This man needs an awakening. The most precious guide within him will only be awakened by a spiritual renewal that will shake him awake. Remove his blinders. Clear his vision. Will he ever learn? Will he ever wake up? Will he ever see clearly again? Will he continue to commit himself to lies or make a new commitment that will change his life's direction forever? The truth will tell with time.

Lies of Omission

A lie of omission is quite different from a lie of commission. It is more difficult to determine with lies of omission if they are true lies. This type of lie withholds details and information. The person you're lying to is hidden from the entire truth. This omission can be for good reason or for bad.

A person may omit truth for several reasons: to protect themselves from a consequence, to protect someone else, or to escape personal responsibility for their actions.

Whether or not omitting the truth is acceptable depends on the intent of the person doing it. For example, if someone was to withhold information by accident, that would not be a situation where they intended to lie or hide the truth. They may have just forgotten or didn't pay attention to the details. This is not a lie. It is just forgetfulness.

Withholding details of a situation or inappropriate content to protect the innocent is another example. The intent is not to harm, but to protect the innocent. This is an acceptable lie by omission with the intent to protect others from harm. This can easily be seen in families with younger children. Parents protecting their children may not go into all the details about certain topics. This technically falls within a lie of omission but is acceptable by any good parent. Though this falls within the category of lying, it's not a true lie. It is protecting. Outright lying by omission, to be a real lie, must be determined to be a lie by intent. This is true even if the intent was planned or spontaneous. Intent determines if what is said or done is a lie or not. Forgetting is just not knowing. Protecting the innocent is not lying, it is protecting. It is used to keep someone safe from harm and to shield someone from something potentially dangerous. Even when you may have to withhold information, this falls within the area of protection. It is not lying.

Escaping the reality of life's hardships by sheltering a child can only go on for so long. This usually ends before they begin entering adulthood. What hardships in life should parents protect their children from? Any that would cause emotional, social, mental, or spiritual harm and trauma.

Parents may often overlook how life impacts children emotionally, socially, and spiritually. Though it may be impossible to shield your child from all of life's hardships, there are some things we can do to control and minimize the damage. Reducing the damage is within our reach. This happens with our words and in our actions. It is within the example that we set and model for our children to follow. It's in how we accept or deny the truth. It's in how we accept or deny lies. Are we open and honest with them or are we living a lie? Do we protect them or expose them?

A true lie of omission that is unacceptable is when you withhold evidence or details to protect yourself. This would mislead others about wrongful actions and mischievous behaviors. To lie by omission to protect yourself, or to escape personal responsibility for something you have done wrong is a true lie. It is a true mark of immaturity for a man. It's immature to not take full responsibility for your actions and to look for an easier way out. It's also a real lie to omit facts just to protect yourself.

We don't always know the full intent of why a person lies and does what they do. We don't know what they were thinking or their true intent while lying. In determining "the why" information is being withheld, we often can determine if omitting that information was justified or not. It is never justifiable to lie to avoid negative consequences.

There is something within our nature as human beings that likes taking the easy way out of things. We like the shorter path. The shortest distance between two points is always a straight line, but it is not often practical or moral. It is not the path to maturity, either. The way we grow is by growing through challenges. We must be willing to go the extra distance and to do what is right. Accept personal responsibility.

There were many times in my life, while being truthful and honest, that it worked out far better than I had previously imagined. The key was that I was willing to take responsibility, no matter the consequence. It wasn't always that way for me. I had to learn the hard way.

I will never forget when I was young and stole a candy bar at a local grocery store. I didn't have a motive for doing it except that I wanted to see if I could do it. At that moment I saw that I could do it but so did others. The cops came and so did my parents. I thought I was going to jail. I was scared to death and was given a big scolding. After that incident, I never stole anything again. I learned my lesson. I was able to make amends by apologizing to the store owner. My father paid for the candy bar but made me pay for it many times over.

As a teenager, I found a lost wallet on the side of the road with a lot of money in it and I immediately turned it in. Yes, without taking the money. The police officers were surprised and my credibility with them restored. It felt good to do the right thing. To be honest, I still wish there was no identification in the wallet. Because there was, I knew it didn't belong to me and someone else had worked hard for that money.

We can grow in those moments where we make right what we have done wrong. This growth is seen by eventually making the correct choices.

Men and boys, both learning to be men, like to avoid things that are difficult. They avoid feelings, some unpleasant activities, and sometimes even telling the truth. The decisions made in life's foxholes determine not only their potential growth but the path they will ultimately follow in life. Each decision is a choice that defines our path of destiny.

Choose to lie, choose the truth, or maybe a little of both. Whatever you decide, the freedom is yours to make, but the results are not yours to choose. Every decision we freely make comes with consequences. The consequences will be either positive or negative. They will help us grow and become better men, or the consequences of our choices will hold us back. These decisions will thrust us forward in life, or they will just tie us down. It's your choice!

Black lies, white lies, and gray lies: they are all lies. The color of a lie doesn't make it any different from a lie just because you colored it. It is still what it is. Just like there is no difference between human beings based on the color of their skin, they are still human beings with equal value.

Martin Luther King Jr. encouraged us that we shouldn't judge a person by the color of their skin, but the content of their heart. We should never value or devalue someone based on their skin color. Doing so is a lie! What matters most is the intent of their heart. In the same way, we can't judge a lie based on its color, only the intent. It's always the intent and reason why someone lied by omission that makes all the difference. While the intent of omitting the truth determines if it's a real lie or not, the decision of committing an actual lie is always one.

The Light Was Not on Yet

There was a young boy who grew up in a home where he had to fend for himself. His clothes seemed to be too small on him. The socks he wore had holes in them. There was always food for him to eat but not the extras he saw others had. He didn't have nice things. This young man often desired to have extra money like other kids and to be able to buy something fun to play with. He was a smart kid and spent a lot of time outside looking for things to do. He found a local Boy Scout troop. It was just the thing that helped him to stay occupied. He enjoyed it a lot. He was a talker and loved being around others. He was excited when he was asked to sell some light bulbs to raise money for the Scouts. What he didn't like was the two-dollar price tag they were selling them for. This kid knew he could sell them for much more. He also believed that he should be compensated for his time while helping the Boy Scouts. He sold them for four dollars and pocketed half the money. He was never caught. He sold a few dozen cases and made some decent cash. This scout lied to himself that this situation was justified. When it was time to turn in all the money he collected, he omitted the fact that he collected more for himself and only turned in what was expected of him. He was immature and didn't think that he was stealing money. It didn't belong to him. He was a volunteer helping the Scouts raise money. They had asked him to help them, not himself. He was supplied with light bulbs. They didn't belong to him, and they were not his to sell the way he wanted.

He had agreed to collect revenue for the Boy Scouts at a certain price and later he left out information that would have given him unfavorable consequences. He stole money from the people who were purchasing the light bulbs and lied, by omission, about it to protect his actions. He was wrong.

Maturity is not something you can get away from. It will wait for you. If you choose to continue participating in immature behaviors and lies, you will continually be faced with repeated obstacles to overcome. A man who always has to get his way will face many challenges. Getting angry and throwing a fit may have worked before but it is immature. A man needs to realize that he won't always get his way. Until he does realize this, he will continuously be confronted with situations that arouse that childish anger. These obstacles will always be harder when you don't handle them correctly. When you learn to do what is correct, the situation may still be there, but it will be easier to manage. You learn good coping techniques. It may eventually, even seem to disappear.

When my daughter was little, she was determined to master the monkey bars before the end of summer. Every time we brought her to the park, she made a beeline straight to the monkey bars. In the beginning, she started across the monkey bars and made it only two bars before falling off. Her determination and practice paid off. Each day she grew stronger and more agile. Every day she added more progress towards her goal. Eventually, she completed the task and conquered the monkey bars as summer ended. This determination and drive to succeed we proudly see in her today.

Men need to be determined to grow up. To be mature men.

Stop hiding your lies behind all your immaturity. Grow up and change into the man others need you to be.

Practice always makes you better at what you're practicing, except for failure. You can't practice failure. It's what happens when you give up totally. It's what you become when you stop improving. Maturity lessons to keep growing are inevitable. I have met some very mature twenty-year-old young men and some "really" immature senior citizens. You can't avoid growing up! You only can delay it.

Growing by Choice

Not taking the correct responsibility that is expected of you at any age is immaturity. We can exhibit immaturity in many ways; emotionally, mentally, physically, spiritually, and relationally.

As we age there is a natural expectation. At the same level of physical maturity, we expect a person will also mature in other areas. This is not a realistic expectation to have since we all will grow, or not grow, from the choices we make and the responsibilities we carry or accept.

Life throws us enough challenges to train us. These challenges provide the necessary opportunities to develop. As we age, we usually have enough life encounters that challenge us to develop maturity. This all depends on how we handle each life situation.

Eventually, a young person may have to deal with losing an animal or a relative. Depending on how important the loss was to the individual, will determine the degree of hardship they will have to endure. How meaningful the relationship was to them will determine how they choose to handle this crisis in their life. The level of emotional and social intelligence they have will be challenged. If he is immature emotionally, he may find ways to ignore how he is feeling. He may never learn to identify those feelings and deal with them correctly. This could cause him to develop some strong negative coping mechanisms to avoid his emotions and never fully mature. As time goes on and his negative coping mechanisms build, he may continue to resist growing. Even though the degree and level of pain have also systematically increased it becomes a subconscious reflex.

Mixed emotions can make you angry when grieving a loss. It is important to identify and learn from how you are feeling. Instead of feeling stuck in your loss, obsessing over wanting more time with a loved one, you can learn to cherish the memories you had. As you learn to identify how you are feeling, you will learn to be open and honest with yourself. This will help guide you through the grieving process. Emotionally, you will grow and mature. Hopefully, you will grow to realize the benefit of identifying and sharing your feelings appropriately and will continue to benefit from it. If you block your feelings, you will be stuck, especially emotions associated with grief. It will stall and wait for you to face it again when you are ready and honest with how you are feeling. Grief does take its own time and it is different for everyone. Be patient with yourself and others.

I was so young and extremely immature. I didn't have many good examples to follow. It's not always a good thing when your motto is, "I will just do the opposite of everything I saw my father do." In some ways, that mindset paid off, but it didn't prepare me to handle my immaturity. That was mine to handle all alone. Father or no father. A good example or not. I was bound to discover that it was something only I could deal with. No one could do it for me. No one could prepare me for what I would experience. Others could offer advice and share their personal experiences that could help me. In the end, it was my life to live. This was my ride to take, my choices to make, and my place to grow, or not grow. I was so young I didn't know how to handle or process my emotions. I didn't know the right way to act or the correct things to say. This had a great impact on my relationships.

I remember dating my wife for the first time as high school sweethearts. I just knew one thing; I liked her, a lot! She was not too impressed with the dozens of stuffed animals that I spent hours trying to win at the mall arcade. Who said, "it's the thought that counts"? She was not an easy catch. I tried to continually impress her with foolishness. Seeing her was challenging. Her father saw this as an opportunity to get some work done around his house. I remember hours of long work just to get an hour with her at dinner with the family. This did make me appreciate her more. At that time, I thought I was just working for additional time to spend with her. But it was teaching me that there are things in this life of higher value that do not come easy. She was the princess, and I was the frog. I don't know what she saw in me. We became best friends.

High School ended and I decided to join the Army. This would prove to be a challenge that required me to grow up relatively fast. I had to make decisions to grow socially, mentally, emotionally, and relationally. I am not saying that the military always helps people to grow and mature but for me, it helped.

It offered me the structure and confidence I needed at that time. It was a good decision and far better than joining the mafia. My family had been a part of the mafia for generations before me. Upon returning from the military, my best friend and future wife were waiting for me. Who can resist a man in uniform anyway? After several years, her gamble with me seemed to pay off. We got married.

I still had a lot of maturing to do. She saw "potential." Potential can be a dangerous and wonderful thing. It profoundly means you can change. How you change is yet to be determined. I was about to make some life-altering decisions. I was on a journey to learn, to grow, and to mature. Each decision would determine my future. Who I was to become. I will never regret the path I took. In hindsight, I never knew how much I was about to change. It may seem odd but there were many times when I felt that I had completely changed one hundred percent. This has happened several times in my life. It came because of a changed mindset and adapting to life principles. It caused me to grow and mature. I had learned something on a spiritual journey that completely revolutionized my thinking. It challenged me to be a better man and to be truthful. I faced the lies that held me back and embraced the truth.

Facing life and its challenges cause men to come toe to toe with their personal development. The potential is there. Will you improve or stay stuck? Will you dig your heels in where you are, or take a step forward?

I never realized how much I had to still grow and learn. At some point, after our second child, I looked back on my life. Once again, I realized how much I had changed, and how much I had grown. At this time in my life, I learned to communicate and relate better than I had ever done before. I could have stayed the way I was, but I didn't want to be like my father. I wanted to be the best father I could be to my children and live up to my wife's high expectations and the potential she saw in me. I learned to understand how I felt and how to handle my emotions. My past wounds and failures were exposed and presented me often with opportunities to deal with them. Like the layers of an onion, things of my past started to peel off. A little here. A little there. As I faced things that needed changing, I would face the issues I was confronted with while peeling off another layer of the past. As time went on other life challenges would eventually give me more opportunities to peel off more of my immaturity.

Hardships were still hard to deal with. In each one, we decided to face it together and it would bring us closer together rather than farther apart. Eventually, what we learned from these challenges transformed us so much. We learned to work together. We began thinking the same thoughts, feeling the same way about things, and wanting the same things in life. We have heard others say, "Just deal with it." That's what it takes to grow. We began dealing with life's challenges and taking the personal responsibility necessary in each situation that came our way.

Some of life's challenging situations will get easier to deal with. Others will be harder and demand more determination. The choices we make to grow will stretch us, and that is a good thing. Harder challenges may be too difficult to handle all alone. We may need to ask for help from friends or professionals who have more experience dealing with these situations. This increases our emotional, social, and relational intelligence when we reach out for help. A man may realize the benefit of multiple views to be effective. This can be very beneficial and healthy for his future relationships.

A Dangerous Defense

When an immature man does not want to deal with something that they are confronted with, one way he may choose to deal with it is to lie. This is the worst way to deal with challenges as it completely disregards the situation. Lying is an act of immediate denial. It is an immature solution for those with underdeveloped skills. It's a way to quickly dismiss something by taking the easy way out. This is rather than taking the harder and more challenging way. When a man lies, he is not taking the higher road in life. He is living on a low road that won't get him far. Lies may promise easy success, but they are just like so-called "get rich quick" schemes. They promise you easy success and financial independence. They slowly take away from you your time and independence. This keeps you from the more important things in life. Only the ones who started those pyramid "lies" profit financially from them, but their time to pay up will come.

Personal development is a slow and steady process. Trying to make quick changes will not last. The sooner a man begins to be honest and deal with his insecurities, the closer he gets to resolution and growth.

There is a problem with today's society. Many people are comfortable pretending problems in their life are not there. It is a culturally accepted atmosphere where playing video games for hours and hours exists. They use this virtual world as a means of escape from the harshness of the real world. These people escape to a reality where the challenges they face are not their own. It is a world where they can overcome these challenges. Here they feel they can escape from the challenges that await them in real life. In the virtual world, life and death often come and go extremely fast. There is no time to reflect on these changes as you must adapt "On the fly". These people are otherwise known as Avatars in games and are a digital representation of the person playing. They are continuously leveling up by gaining experience or completing objectives. Players also increase their skills to face the next challenge as well as find equipment to improve their character's power. While playing as someone else, these players don't get to know who they "really" are. Instead, they often are just pretending to be someone else or are just a hollow shell in virtual reality. For these people, there is no reason to deal with the harshness of the real world. Living in a virtual world means there is no time to deal with real emotions and grow in the real world. They can become emotionally numb, relationally petrified, and spiritually stunted. This can also be true for those who lose themselves in movies, books, tv shows, as well as other entertainment. They become oblivious to their "own" reality while living in the virtual reality of their own making. Limiting themselves. Under Experienced. These people never learn to make the necessary changes in the real world to develop a true understanding of themselves. The truth is that video games and other entertainment can serve a purpose as a temporary means of escape, if you understand that you must disconnect and deal with the real world. An example of this is the Pandemic of 2020. During this time of lockdown, many people wanted to escape the horrors of quarantine and chose a virtual means of escape. False realities can help cope with your hardship if you do not ignore your real life. Be sure you do not let it control your life.

Growth is essential for all healthy relationships. Living a fantasy lie can have a tremendous impact on your life. It can keep you from developing the skills necessary for proper interaction in relationships. Learning to deal with emotions appropriately is key to being open to new real-life adventures. The lie of fantasy robs you of these adventures. We all start somewhere. We start from where we are and work to be more. To be better than who we are today. To learn. To grow. To change. It's time to stand up and be a man. Take the personal responsibility that is yours to take. Make decisions that push you into growing for better and not for worse. Decide to always be open, to learn, and to grow towards maturity.

Don't give in to the divisiveness of lies. They promise you an easy way out, but leave you with broken relationships, shattered dreams, and living as an immature man. Don't hide behind a fantasy lie that may seem fun now but has little real-life application.

An Easy Mistake

Mistakes. We all make them from time to time, but we don't always take responsibility for them. Taking responsibility for your actions is a sign of growth and maturity. Avoiding responsibility because of the negative consequences will carry over into every other area of your life. It is also the definition of immaturity. It's amazing how avoiding responsibility can seem easier at first but in the end, it robs you of more than you will ever know. Don't let lying and avoiding responsibility carry over into not being a responsible parent, employee, or citizen. It costs too much. The price you pay to lose a relationship with your children, your wife, and your friends is not worth it. Start today to be honest and take responsibility for your actions every day.

When I was seventeen years old, I had a part-time job at a repair shop washing cars. Some days were nice, but most days the weather was cold. This was why they kept the big overhead doors closed. One day, I was asked to move a car inside to help a mechanic. My instructions were to get the car, open the garage's automatic door, and then close the door after pulling the car inside. I got most of this right. When I pulled the car in and closed the overhead door, the car was not far enough in. The repair shop was big enough for this mistake to go unnoticed. I knew it was only a matter of time since there was a big dent in the garage door. I was young and just wanted to hide what had happened. Maybe they would think someone else did it. If I said nothing, no one would ever know. I will only know. It was an accident anyway.

Lies and deceit started playing in my mind. I had a choice to make. I could continue to play this lying game in my mind or take responsibility for what I did. If I chose to lie, I may have to defend that lie with more lies.

I decided to go to my supervisor and tell him what happened and come clean. He had a good laugh, and eventually fixed the door. I had anticipated getting fired or having to pay for the repairs. In the end, all that happened was a few good laughs and a new nickname.

Please don't think taking responsibility for your actions will always turn out so easy. I lucked out that time at the shop. It did teach me that the stress and mind manipulation of lying is a lot worse than being honest and telling the truth. I was growing and maturing as a man and building a reputation of being honest.

I had a job many years later as a rehabilitation counselor for an addiction center where a situation came up. I was confronted by a supervisor who asked me if I forgot to do some paperwork. It was up to my word alone. There was no way to prove it. I told the truth. I forgot to submit the necessary paperwork and I apologized. This made my supervisor's job more difficult because she had to give an account of my negligence. It inadvertently made her trust me more. When I was later accused of doing something I had not done, she stood by my reputation and my character. Eventually the truth came out. The person that had accused me admitted they lied. This person was just trying to get me in trouble because they did not like a recommendation I had made. They didn't want to face the consequences and lied to avoid them. Think about the same situation if I had a history of lying and not taking personal responsibility. Immaturity could have cost me more than just my job. No one would have trusted me. Confusion, misunderstanding, and suspicion would have tainted my words. Lies need more lies to keep a lie going. It would have undermined my relationships. Eventually you will find yourself in a place where no one trusts you and people are cautious of you, showing little support.

Honesty, truth, and trust are like bridges. They support

healthy relationships. One of the biggest compliments I ever received was from this supervisor who had my back. She said to the accuser, "If you knew him, you would know that's not possible for him to do." My previous decisions and truthful actions followed me. They protected me. It was like a bridge that was built and was there when I needed it most.

We choose our reputation through our actions. It is what others count on when they give us the benefit of doubt. It's a benefit because you doubt the allegations and accusations from the lying of others. There will always be those who want to tarnish a good reputation. Perhaps they are jealous. If you have been honest and truthful your reputation will stand. Being honest and not lying will give you a good reputation. The problem lies in the fact that it is harder to build a good reputation once you have tarnished it rather than just maintaining it when it was good. This is what every man must live with. No matter where your reputation is today, you can always take steps to improve it. You could improve from the mistakes you made if you chose to do so. You must make the time to be honest and mature. You must take responsibility for your life and your reputation. You can be the man you were meant to be and who others need you to be. Don't be bogged down by life events but let them be used as a catalyst for your growth into true manhood. If you find yourself working on a new reputation due to your past mistakes, be patient with yourself and with others. Growth is gradual and so is trust.

Some people will trust you right away. They are usually new friends you have just met. There may be others who understand what you're going through. They may have a similar experience. There will be those who will be watching you before they decide to trust you again. They want to see if you will stay steady and truthful. Will this change last? When you finally prove to them you have changed, they will be your biggest supporters.

There will be others who will never trust you again. Your old reputation and mistakes may have hurt them too deeply. Even if you prove to them, you are a new person all together, it won't help. The issue is not with you anymore, it's with them. You must let this go so it does not hold you back. The best thing you can do is continue to grow and to be the best honest and mature version of you that you can be. Become your new honest self with a shiny new reputation to prove it. Be who you were meant to be. Sometimes there will be situations in life that can't be resolved. They are out of your control. Someone else's lies tarnished your good reputation in their own estimation. It could be that pride has blinded others from seeing the entire truth and they choose to believe the part that makes you look bad. It's hardest when it comes from those who should know who you are. There is not much you can do but to take things slow, be humble, accept any part of responsibility that may be yours, and be authentic as possible. You can't change other people or their opinions; only they can do that for themselves.

Questions for Self-Reflection

What immature things do you still struggle with?

How have you committed a lie with misleading intent recently?

How have you omitted the truth to defend yourself or your actions?

Have you omitted the truth to protect those you love? How?

Would you rather, in omitting truth, protect yourself or others? Explain.

5

A Fragmented Image

Who am I? This is a question everyone asks themselves at some point in their life. The search for inward truth often can be seen in how you search for meaning and how you search for purpose in life. How you see yourself can have both a positive and a negative impact on your life depending on your perspective. How you view yourself will determine how you think, act, and relate with others. Your image is not something that can always be outwardly noticed. You may look at someone and think, "Wow, they are full of themselves." When In reality, it is all just a facade to hide what is going on deep inside themselves.

Many people use distractions to draw their attention away from how they really feel about themselves. It's how one internally views themself that matters most, not the interference they are running through distraction. It's not how you dress or don't dress, the tattoos or piercings covering your body, your excess makeup or lack thereof, or your odd acting behavior. That's all just an attempt to cover up the truth of who you "really" are. Your thoughts and feelings are the true lenses of how you see the world and primarily your place in it. It is also the source of who you are and of what you are meant to be. This can be a lifelong pursuit.

Many people automatically get this image of themselves from their parents. This can be a good or bad image depending on the family you had and the messages they continually spoke and modeled. A good parent would impart an image of confidence, honesty, security, and acceptance. A bad parent might impart an image of fear, failure, lying, insecurity, and abandonment. Not everyone receives the message sent by their parents. It's not always the constant message that grabs you and forms your image. It's more about how you respond to each message sent to you that matters most. Sometimes you must do like the old song says to do and just "Return to Sender." How do you respond? Do you tend to attract or detract? Ingest the subtle cues or totally or partially dismiss them? Do you tend to influence others or are you more easily influenced by them? Even if you were able to turn some negative messages around in your favor, there still may remain some stronger messages deep down that are attached to your self-image. It happens subconsciously. These messages may have been hiding in the dark shadows of your psyche just waiting for you to try to define yourself another way. They are waiting to push you back. Deep down you believed the lie that someone told you. It may have been programmed in you for years that you're a nobody and you believed it. You may have felt worthless and unimportant. No matter what you do in life this message seems to self-sabotage any success you start to have. Somehow, it just stuck.

An image is how someone views themselves. Someone with a fragmented image has a view of themself that is marred by past thoughts, feelings, or actions. This may be observable by themselves or others. It depends on where this view came from. The thoughts, feelings, and actions that surround a fragmented image can also be self-induced through one's behaviors. It can be forced on through the words or actions of others. It's hard to survive and cope with a fragmented image. Often the shame of past mistakes remains a constant reminder that continues to haunt many people. Many will do whatever they can to cover it up, like lying, drinking, using drugs, overworking, and hiding. They will do whatever they can, so they don't have to deal with feeling a certain way about themselves or how others make them feel.

Others have just completely accepted the lie and given in to the fragmented image. If you don't like what you see in the world, start by looking in the mirror just like the song from 1988, "Man in The Mirror" suggests. We all need to start by changing who we are to make a difference in the world. Change starts within your heart. This will reflect what you see in your own image.

We need wholesome men and women who know who they are and what they are. Men that are healed from the wounds left by their father can become great fathers themselves. Women free from bad father figures who now know their worth and are secure. When we are not crippled by a fragmented image, we can embrace our "true" identity. We can reach our full potential. Some are developing into a person whose words and actions are a benefit to those around them. We need to see ourselves in such a way that the people in our lives will love and need us. Be someone they want to be around. It's time to dismember how we used to see ourselves and gain a fresh perspective of who and what we truly are. We need things to be put back into order the right way. The truthful way. It's time to be whole. We can't just be a piece of who we are meant to be. We need to be the entire package others need by embracing integrity and not being divided within. Men and women that are whole, sound, and of utmost character are a true asset to those near them. They can now rise and help others all around them.

Florida International University is in Miami, Florida. It's a large university with a bustling city surrounding it. Concern for student safety quickly increased after one college student lost his life crossing the busy intersection that goes through the university property. The idea to build a bridge over the roadway was unanimously accepted. FIU's Engineering Department would spearhead the construction of this bridge. The projected budget for this project was over 19 million dollars. They wanted to design something that would not only be practical but also a landmark, an architectural achievement. This would provide their engineering department with the credibility it needed to attract more engineering students for years to come. In the end, the university ended up only spending 9 million dollars building the bridge. The bridge was mainly constructed as a post-tensioned concrete bridge and was supposed to last 100 years and withstand a Category 5 hurricane.

Concrete is a building material often used for its strength and durability. This monumental bridge design included a concrete walkway and a covering over the walkway that was also made from concrete. It was to be 320 feet long and would weigh 950 tons. The center beam of the suspension cables and supports would brace this massive structure. The department of transportation had instructed them to move a support so they could add another traffic lane later on. The plans had to be revised to accommodate these last-minute changes. What was not taken into proper consideration, by a licensed engineer, was how moving the support and cables 11 feet would fully impact this project. The engineering department tried to limit traffic congestion by constructing concrete pieces for the bridge on each side of the road. They would then later move them into place. Minor cracks were originally expected when moving concrete pieces. This bridge was meant to showcase the engineering department's crowning achievement. Unbeknownst to them, this plan was now fragmented even before it began. Five days after it was moved into place, no one could have known what was going to happen. How could they know that there was a fatal design flaw? The minor cracks were much larger than projected. They were forty times larger than what was acceptable. That which was meant to protect, and help was fragmented from its intended purpose and image. This bridge was meant to assist students in crossing the intersection safely, but it had severe integrity issues. These issues not only collapsed the bridge but took 6 innocent lives of unsuspected people and severely injured 10 others. Many years later, they are still pointing fingers as to who is to blame for this Titanic Bridge.

On the contrary, in Upstate New York, there is a small town called Herkimer where there is a concrete bridge that is still standing that was built in 1903. It was a trolley bridge that was only operational for thirty years. This concrete structure was over 1200 feet long. This arched trolly bridge was built so well that it has outgrown its intended purpose and still stands over a hundred years later. What a legacy! The FIU pedestrian bridge was three times smaller than this trolley bridge which lasted way longer than five days. This abandoned trolley bridge stands as a testament to its integrity and design.

In the same way today, we have fathers, mothers, husbands, wives, and friends who are meant to protect, help, and strengthen others' lives. They are meant to be our bridge to help us get where we are going in life. Some have lacked integrity. They have allowed, into their hearts and minds, a fragmented image of how they see themselves. This fragmented image has caused much damage to the lives of others. Their wives thought they were honest but have been hurt by their lies. Their innocent children depended on them to lead them to a better place in life, only to find themselves hurt and confused. Their husbands thought they had a future together only to realize, after 20 years, they were not enough to feed her sexual appetite. Their friends couldn't depend on them anymore. These men and women have fallen like a bridge, caused damage, and need to be rebuilt. Their lives are in pieces. They don't possess the soundness of character needed to sustain a storm or to endure pressure. The weight of responsibility has proven to be too much. They never allowed themselves to develop inwardly the honorable character needed. They need to be transformed from the faulty image that was placed on them that they ultimately accepted.

Life sends us tests. Our choices and decisions during these tests determine the person we become. Can you go through a circumstance while consistently maintaining a good attitude? Are you a person that others can depend on? Can you maintain your honorable character when life gets tough? Are you ok with Lying? "This is where the rubber meets the road." This is where the person we become through these tough times will undergo an examination. The hardships we face in life determine if our character is real or if we are just pretending. If it's real, it will stick and remain. But if we are lying to ourselves, we will stop pretending when things get too difficult. Is the transformation truly real? Can our patience last through tough situations? If it can, it will prove to be something genuine. Our character becomes honorable, whole, sound, and dependable. This is the very character that those close to us can depend on. It is what those who depend upon us need to help them grow and develop into who they are meant to be.

Character traits are like the ingredients in concrete. Sand, water, cement, and gravel are mixed to make concrete. This is just like when different positive character traits are combined. Mixing trust, love, faithfulness, honesty, patience, joy, self-control, kindness, and peace form a bond that can withstand hurricane-like winds in our life and relationships. They help to build family legacies. Character. One trait left all alone is not enough. It must join with the other traits and then be tested with time, and through hardships, to be genuine. This is to make sure it is pure and not mixed with anything negative. Character should not be mixed with amounts of arrogance, selfish ambition, unfaithfulness, addiction, perversion, greed, and hatred. These negative traits added to your life will make you impure and even dangerous. It will transform you into something different and, maybe, even unexpected. You will be weakened from the inside and ready to fail in life and in your relationships. You become someone else, something else. People who allow these negative traits are impeded by a fragmented image. They are working against what they are meant to be. When concrete fails due to being exposed to something harmful to its chemical structure it is called concrete degradation. When men and women are exposed to harmful mindsets, attitudes, and actions, the very image of who they are truly meant to be is at risk while giving into self-degradation. This causes damage in their life just like crumbling concrete. It not only hurts themselves but those who trusted them. The pain they cause others is often too hard to bear, especially upon those they love and care for. Many may often try to hide behind life's vices of drugs, alcohol, or lies that society offers to them to mask the truth. People may have struggles they are dealing with that are, little by little, being purged from their identity and image. Some people are alright living with an internal flawed design that hurts themselves and others. They may feel they don't have much to offer. They are lying to themselves about their true potential because they are really meant to be a hero and not a zero.

A hero is defined as someone admired for their outstanding achievements and their courage. A hero is a man or woman of truth. He is a man not permanently stuck in the past pain left by a bad father figure. She is a woman not permanently stuck in the past pain left by a bad father or mother figure. They have been healed from the pain of their past by accepting true forgiveness. They can now look in the mirror and see their real image unmarred from their past. They have unlocked unlimited potential. This has freed them to embrace who they were always meant to be - Heroes.

Super Dad

From the first moment I held each of my precious little children in my arms, I realized something. They were extremely fragile, vulnerable, and innocent.

The day I became a father I decided that I would do whatever it takes to be the strength they will always need. The day you became a father is the day you became your child's superhero. That's the day you put on the cape to become "super dad." What others think of you no longer matters. Now, you mean the world to the life you're holding in your arms.

Nothing could have prepared you for such an honor. Being a father, one could never imagine what it would be like until that day came. You envisioned yourself protecting your child long before they were born. Now as you hold them in your hands, they see you as the strongest person in the world. You are their father.

How will you use that strength? How will it be defined? In the early stages of child development, you prove your strength by carrying them everywhere, taking care of their needs, and with every hug. Mere physical strength alone won't protect them.

Some people who describe their dad as primarily physically strong also see him as someone who pushes his weight around. They define him as a bully and someone who always gets their own way. Some men are bullies because they don't know how to act appropriately. They don't know how to exchange their physical strength for internal power.

Some men draw their strength from their mental capacity or knowledge. Early on, they start teaching and training their children to learn things to be just like them. They put all their effort into their child's mental aptitude and preparedness. This is not bad, but focusing on knowledge alone can send the wrong message. The message received is that they will never measure up and are never going to be good enough for dad. As their father keeps placing his expectations higher and higher, children may struggle to keep up and seem to sometimes fall short. Some children just give up, and others later regret everything they missed out on during their childhood. This, while trying to keep up with dad's mental challenges and physical expectations of a workaholic. Physical strength and mental aptitude are good things for children to have, but they are not the main characteristics that will protect your child. If men are not careful, their strength that is meant to help will be used to cause pain and frustration. With great strength comes great responsibility. Some men have figured out how to master their superpower by defining their strength through character. This strength is often revealed by their interactions with their children and how they talk to them. This can also be seen in how he treats their mother and interacts with others in society.

As hard as it may be, opening his mouth to tell his children how much they mean to him and how much he loves them displays strength through gentleness and respect.

There is a strength in his humility. He doesn't see himself as better than anyone else, but he also doesn't see himself as less than anyone else either. His children follow his example as it has been modeled to them. You must choose how you will demonstrate your strength. You may demonstrate your strength as being mentally or physically strong, or it can be demonstrated through gentleness and showing respect. When you are under great pressure and struggling with adversity your true choice is often revealed.

Your superhero power is your ability to create the very foundation your children need to stand on. Dads everywhere have a choice. They can be a superhero or a villain. Don't be a villain dad who controls the life of others by overpowering them. This villain is twisted in his thinking and has an internal picture of himself that is fragmented. He needs to control others to feel in control. Controlling others, especially your children, will not produce a loving response, only regret. It will stifle your kids and produce in them unintended hardship.

Fathers should set an example for their children to follow. If he chooses to display a bad example, he will offer a cracked and broken foundation for his children to build on. His strength will break the very life he should have protected.

The mental villain continues to prove how much his children can't measure up to his standards and leaves some of them with regrets in need of repair. He cripples them with his high expectations. Shutting them down mentally, these children become immovable in life and are set up to experience an even greater fall later in life, especially emotionally.

Super dad's strength is in the preparation and security he offers his children. Then they can embrace the qualities that can be built upon with a solid and strong foundation for their lives. He knows how to use his physical strength in moderation. His mental capacity with balance. He has developed the character to be a great protector. He knows how to pass along what he has learned.

The Guardian Dad

In our world, pain and suffering are everywhere. Innocent lives are ruined, and addictions have taken many lives. Slavery is still an issue as it has been for centuries. Secret sex slaves in vast amounts are hidden behind closed doors. It is a cancer that plagues our society. Many young people run away from home to escape one bad place just to end up in another bad place: or somewhere worse. Others find themselves struggling with drug use only later to be bound to addiction. Many people are blind and can't see the injustice that's happening. Only recently have some eyes been awakened to the horror of death caused by overdose. What once seemed like innocent experimentation has grown into an uncontrollable obsession near death's door. Just a tiny drop of two milligrams of Fentanyl will kill you. That's just equivalent in size to five grains of salt; just a sprinkle. While our society has taken some notice of the struggle of addiction, they remain blind towards the horrors of sex slavery around the world. Many of our big cities are home to this multi-billion-dollar industry that is being built by taking away the life of others who are often still children themselves. Where is true justice in our society? Where have all the protectors gone? It starts in our homes where dad is on the scene. This man was not sent to be the protector of the world, but to protect his family's heart and life. To do this, he needs to use his superpowers to create a barrier of physical and emotional protection around his family, so they won't be harmed. His first responsibility is to his home, making sure his family are safe and protected. He helps them make wise choices, so they are not put in harmful situations. Guiding them to see the bigger picture that's developed from his life experience.

He is the spiritual leader of their home and sets the example of a healthy spiritual life. He knows he cannot protect his family alone and relies on the guidance of God to help him navigate where he cannot see or be. It's like he is taking them on a hike where the trail has already been marked out by the forest ranger who knows the rough terrain. The Ranger walks ahead of each trail placing markers on trees where it is safe to travel. In his spirituality he just needs to keep in focus where the trail markers are. He and his family need to just stay on the correct path. Otherwise, they risk more harm than was ever intended in their life. Guardian Dad protects his family from forces, unseen and seen, that want to hold them back and keep them bound by different types of negative social thinking. He helps them build security and trust, so they know who they are and the family that they are a part of. He protects their hearts and minds, keeping them open to faith, hope, and love, while not bound by greed, unforgiveness, and hate. He is the defender of their spiritual and emotional health, keeping them on the path of truth.

When tough times come, they can count on him for help. He works continuously to keep them feeling safe. He creates an environment where they can relax and be at peace without having to think about all the evil in the world around them.

The Guardian Dad will be able to keep fighting injustice, long after his children have grown up themselves. If they need him, he is there. Life is not fair, and he knows this so he stands where injustice happens. He does this to balance things out and make up the difference where things in life are unfair. He knows that life often happens to get hard and throws you out of balance. Then it becomes difficult to make an adjustment by yourself without some help. Like a table with legs that are not balanced will make eating very difficult, but with a slight adjustment from guardian dad things are now aligned and steady.

He is there to protect those who can't protect themselves, protecting the innocent and vulnerable. He is at the forefront of the battle against addiction. He keeps his defenses up by not being someone who uses anything that would make him a vulnerable guardian. He sets the right example for his children's safety. Guardian Dad is there to help keep innocent children safe. When their innocence has been taken unjustly, he is there to help make it right. He does this by supporting the efforts of their freedom when he can. He may be there rescuing them himself or partnering with others that help, while he waits for their return. He is not in this fight alone. He has others there to help. The police officer, judge, social worker, and other moms and dads are there to help.

Either way, he will be there to help them recover from the wounds that have been caused by others. He will be there until their painful wounds change to scars as he helps nurture them back to health. Guardian Dad is a hero who protects his family physically, spiritually, and emotionally by putting up a protective barrier that will help. With these things all in order, he fights injustice, first at home and then abroad. He protects those who can't protect themselves, helps the innocent, and saves lives.

Dependable Man

Sometimes in life we find ourselves having to do things we never planned on doing. That's where I found myself during a global pandemic. Previously, I worked in the financial industry for several years, but I found myself working as a mechanic at our family's car dealership. Why? Simply, because it needed to be done and they needed my help. There are times in life when we do things we really don't want to do because they are necessary. Others need us. It may not be permanent but right now you are needed. Yes, that's how I ended up as a mechanic. My family was going through some tough times during COVID 19 and needed a hand. I jumped in to help. That's what it means to be dependable. To be there when others need you. I don't mean being everything to all people, but you need to be everything to the people that matter most.

It was during this time I learned more than being a mechanic. I realized how some people put the work in to make their vehicle reliable while others don't.

You wake up rushing out the door for work and go to start your car and nothing - the battery is dead. You're at work your first day on the job and after you get out of your car, you notice that you have a flat tire. After a rainstorm, you must run an errand and you drive through a partially flooded road and your engine light comes on. Sometimes it seems like everything is going wrong all at the same time.

How many repairs in a short period of time does it take before you consider getting another vehicle? As soon as possible. Why? Because it's just not dependable anymore. It can't be counted on when you need it most. It always seems to break down when you least expect it, and it makes you feel unprepared. Caught off guard.

One of the worst things someone can say about you as a man is that they can't depend on you. What a slap in the face! A true sign of being responsible as a man is that others can depend on you. After all, your superpower is the ability to be dependable.

Your work loves that they can depend on the fact you are always there, even if you don't wear a cape and can't fly. Family members always praise you for the help you are always willing to give them. Your wife enjoys that when she asks you to do things, you remember to do them and get them done. She is so appreciative of you and grateful to have someone so reliable.

They can count on "Dependaman." He is rock solid in his dependability. If you're a man, then you have this power too. It's a great ability. It builds on your good reputation. That's why I am so surprised that many men don't use this superpower.

They just let life happen to them, without taking responsibility. They don't take the reins in their life that are theirs to hold and say, "giddy-up." They just totally ignore their control of situations.

Instead, they are undependable. This undermines their credibility and does nothing to build a good reputation as a man. Their employer must babysit them because they are not responsible enough to manage their own time. Their wives are frustrated by constantly asking them to do things that never get done.

All this time, their super ability goes unused, sitting dormant. All you need to do is activate it. So why aren't you?

Maybe it's time to trade in that undependable car for one that can be counted on. Dependability creates security. When you know someone is always there for you, it builds your confidence. A vehicle you depend on does not give you a headache. You don't have to think about it much, just get in a go when needed. If you have to worry about your vehicle or man all the time, they are probable not dependable.

Many men can't handle wearing their "super suit" because they are too insecure. Being insecure will tear down any security that is built around you. It's based on a fear that no one will be there for you. It comes from not feeling cared for or loved. There is always this feeling that someone is going to take the good things away, so the insecure man limits himself and puts limits on others around him.

These limits measure the depth of his relationships. He keeps others at a distance because he feels if he lets others in, they may replace him or not need him at all. If he lets them in, they may not like who he really is.

This fear makes him undependable. If he would only put on his super suit and reject insecurity, he would realize the power of his dependability.

Without insecurity, he will see that others are there to help him build stronger, higher, and taller. He will be immune to the lies of insecurity through fear and open to embracing unlimited love. Then, others can count on him, and he can count on others too.

When he is dependable, he builds into the lives of those he loves, adding security, strength, and confidence. They will win because he has their back. They will face life with confidence because he is always with them. They have the strength to take the necessary risks in life, without fear of failing, because he is there for them whenever and wherever they need him.

The Tranquilizer

Have you ever been to a home where it is complete chaos? I don't mean normal life chaos (that is expected), I mean fabricated chaos.

Normal chaos includes things like dog issues, kid issues, and the hectic nature of life. All you can do is manage them the best you can and get a well-needed break, if possible.

Fabricated chaos is the type of chaos that just seems to magically enter the room with some people. They have a way about them that is disruptive, rude, and chaotic. They just don't care. These are not the kind of traits that calm others and bring peace. On the contrary, they upset people and put everyone on edge.

Now I am sure everyone knows someone who seems to carry around chaos with them wherever they go. These people bring and create chaos from within.

Some of them you have already nicknamed "crazy" or "whirlwind." These are not the people you invite over after the kids just went to bed or after a long day at work. You stay away from them and keep your distance. Why? Because they exhaust you mentally and emotionally.

They are Mr. and Mrs. Drano. They drain the best out of you until you have nothing left and nothing more to give. This is when you need to call in The Tranquilizer. He is a real man of peace and can bring people together. He knows how to calm the chaos. This manpower is one all men can, and do have, the ability to carry with them.

They have a way to walk in a room and bring peace. I'm not talking about the stillness and quietness of a "couch potato." That's not peace, that's just taking up space. I'm talking about the presence of peace, a tranquil calmness that he brings with him wherever he is.

You may hardly recognize it. This power often goes unrecognized, as opposed to noticing its nemesis, the villain of chaos. We all notice this villain when he is present. He is a miserable ogre that always has a bad attitude and treats others poorly. He gets attention because he is so disruptive, self-centered, mean, and plain rude.

He has a crazy way about him that makes everyone uneasy. He stirs up trouble and is always looking for a fight. He aims for those in his path who are weak, feeble, and tired. Dealing with him saps all your strength. He is like a vampire that sucks life out of its victims.

The Tranquilizer has a power that is secretive and undercover. That's just how it works. You may not even know he is there until it's time for him to act. He can calm the chaos with his wisdom and guard others against mere exhaustion.

He has a powerful empathy and courage that endures. He cares and it shows in the way he soothes any situation. He is like a human fire extinguisher that can douse and put out the fire of chaos before everything is ruined and destroyed. He exemplifies peace, not laziness.

The Tranquilizer moves forth in corrective action, not in-action. He doesn't sit idly watching but gets involved. He knows that his peaceful actions will benefit those around him. He enjoys taking others to a place of safety and security.

It's in this peaceful environment that others can relax and be themselves. The Tranquilizer works with the guardian to protect others from the lies of pretending to be who they are not. He keeps their minds at ease through peace, so they don't have to worry, (worrying robs peace). His advice and counsel offer a solution that helps you enjoy life to its fullest without worry, and without chaos.

Boredom Buster

No one likes a person that is always so serious and never has any fun. They need the Boredom Busters super ability.

Many moms are a little jealous of this superhero power. You may often hear them say, "you have all the fun and I have to always be the bad guy." Men, especially dads, have the clever ability to have fun with the strangest things. It's a superhero power that brings laughter and joy to a household. They have a way of imparting to us a simple truth - that life is an adventure to be enjoyed and shared.

I will never forget the multiple kickball games, video games, board games, card games, and costumes I enjoyed as a father. We still enjoy many of these games today, minus the costumes.

Memories are built around having fun and enjoying each other's company. While playing a game, something happens. Defense mechanisms begin to fade, and everyone begins to relax. Random conversation starts and laughter often follows. Mild competition adds to the excitement.

This superpower is amazing and fun! It can bypass straight through to the memory center in families.

Many men may be prone to abuse this power. This can be done in two ways: when you become overly competitive while playing games, or when you neglect other responsibilities for fun. Either of these will backfire and create a negative memory.

Be forewarned fathers, with all the video games today you may have to fight for your children's time. Don't fight with your children but be willing to work hard to establish a ritual or a routine that fights for them. The more often you can consistently have fun together, the better it will be. You may have to be willing to change what you think is fun and learn to enjoy something they want to do more.

I know that I love board games, but my son started to love playing card games. They were overly complex and hard to understand. I had to decide, force him to play a board game and be miserable the entire time, or sacrifice some pleasure on my part to learn what he is interested in. So, I invested in it and bought more cards. After playing the card game several times, it became easier, and I started having lots of fun. Most importantly, I was able to spend quality time with my son and build some happy memories that we continue to share.

When you let yourself get too competitive, it always backfires. Don't fall for it. Don't give in to being too competitive, as it takes out all the fun of the game. Instead of the primary focus being quality time and fun, it becomes only about winning.

When you are only focused on the competition, your children become something you overcome, rather than spending time with them. You may feel like a victor, but your crown is cracked.

Too much fun leads to you avoiding your other duties and sends the wrong message - that it is okay to be irresponsible for the sake of having fun.

When fun alone becomes the objective, instead of quality time with your children, they conclude that they are not as important to you. They may even excuse themselves from playing with you because it's more about your pleasure than time spent with them and or fun.

The Boredom Buster knows how to balance the fun he has with his children with his other responsibilities in a way that brings joy to everyone. This may seem like a silly superpower, but when used correctly in balance with your other abilities, it sets you apart as a dad who cares enough to spend time with his children. It makes you a legacy builder as your children remember and rehearse the good times you had together.

The Composer

This is an amazing power that many men have not yet mastered or even tried to use. The Composer's superpower is the ability to control himself in any situation. I am sure many women wish they controlled the on and off switch for this super ability.

Self-control demands moderation. It's the ability to control your thoughts, emotions, and actions before they get out of control. This is done by placing limits on your thoughts and actions. The villain of "being out of control" is trying to gain a position in our mind, thoughts, and actions to exert control over others, which is the opposite mindset to self-control.

Many men have believed the lie that they need to be in control and need to control others when the greatest benefit overall is through controlling themselves. It may feel good to control others sometimes, but it has the least overall benefit in our relationships. Having everyone do exactly what you want them to do is not where you shine as your best. It limits yourself and others.

Creating robotic relationships enslaved from their choices and free will never ends well. It causes these relationships to be void of true love which demands the expression of free will and the power to choose.

Some men don't control others, but instead, they believe a lie that by acting out of control, it will be beneficial in some way. The adrenaline rush they feel from getting out of control often feels good. It can even be addictive.

In many ways it mimics addiction. A man with out-of-control issues has a serious problem. The adrenaline rush is like a drug that is altering his brain chemistry. It becomes such a ritualistic habit that he starts enjoying it more, despite the negative outcomes. It continues long after it has caused much destruction in his life. Despite the negative consequences, he still does not stop doing it and continues in this insanity. Hopefully, he will wise up to what's happening - that he has become an addict of adrenaline.

Controlling others and acting out of control are immature ways to manipulate others to get what you want. When you became a man, it was expected that you put away childish things and take on your new responsibilities. With this great power of yours comes great responsibility. This responsibility and power are contained in controlling yourself, controlling your thoughts, especially your actions.

Self-control over your thoughts is empowering. Many men are slaves to their thought life. They entertain sexual images, situations, and fantasies that demand an outlet. Our thoughts are the seeds planted in our psyche leading towards action.

Eventually, your thoughts and what you think will come out of your mouth. When it has reached a level from thought to speaking it verbally, it's closer to being acted upon. If you don't learn to have self-control in your thinking, you will continually be bound to failure and defeat.

Wanting to have a wonderful marriage, without having a self-controlled thought life, is like wanting to be a bank manager and constantly thinking of robbing the bank. Eventually, an unforeseen opportunity may meet the expectation of your hidden thoughts, leaving you at a crossroads, a decision. This scenario will make it difficult for you to choose correctly. Your decision will have consequences.

Every sexual thought that is out of control creates an avenue for an action that could ultimately hurt your wife, your marriage, and your family. Many men are cheating on their spouse in their thought life.

The difference between thought and action is the consequence of choice. It is easier to see the impact actions have when the consequences are immediate.

It can be difficult to control every thought that comes into your mind. Sometimes we just receive random thoughts. What you do with your thoughts when they do come is what matters most. It's less important what you "actually thought" and more important what you do with it afterward or when it arrives.

There is so much information in our society and it's moving so fast that every male is bound to be bombarded by some image, voice, text, friend request, look, or something that will trigger thoughts that have to be dealt with. To ignore the existence of these thoughts is to subconsciously accept them.

Ask yourself: do you feed on these thoughts and dwell on them? Or do you starve them and intentionally think of something else? The more you exercise this self-control power, you will get better and better at it and your thought life will improve.

Likewise, the more you ignore this power, you will be a man chained to the negative consequences of his thought life. A thought life in time will harvest an action. Actions repeated over time become habits.

I do believe pornography is one of the major downfalls to a good relationship. You may not think so, but pornography has no immediate outlet. It creates a vacuum in your mind that with time and emotion must lead to some action.

Some actions can have major consequences, especially when you have believed a lie that this thought is alright to have. If so, then this emotion is alright to feel. Eventually, you believe this action is alright to choose to do, even if it violates another's rights.

It's time to use your Composer's power of self-control. When you limit negative thoughts and negative thinking, it will help to improve your mood over time with happier emotions. Your actions will be more consistent with who you were meant to be.

Some successful businesspeople have adopted these methods to make more money. They value money over their families. They exercise self-control in their thinking to be a success at making money, instead of being a great husband, father, or friend.

You were meant for so much more than money. You have been given a great responsibility and honor to be a hero to your family. You have the potential power within you to do just that.

Prove your love to them by controlling the things within you that can be destructive to the very relationships you want to build.

Mr. Incredible Love

Once you understand what it is, incredible love is truly an amazing power. The problem in our society is that love has been redefined in ways that we only think about it as something sensual, sexual, and a strong feeling toward someone. This is not what love is. That is just sexual and an infatuation.

A strong feeling towards someone can lead to love, and love may eventually include sex, but we are putting the cart way before the horse.

First and foremost, men must understand the nature and

characteristics of true love to properly use this special ability they have been given. If we as men don't define it correctly, how can we put love to use? How can we know if we are really in love? How do we know if we are loving someone in our life correctly?

In our society today, you must admit, we use the word love rather lightly. We say, "I love that car," "I love chocolate," or "I love pizza." Loosely defining love can create some rather big misconceptions.

What is the difference between loving pizza and loving a spouse? If merely a strong desire to have pizza or to be with someone is your definition of love, then you're not in love. You're in lust.

I wonder how many men today think they are in love when they are in lust? How can you tell the difference? There is one easy test that can tell. Ask yourself an honest question. What's in this for me? What do I want out of this? Lust will always be focused on your wants and needs, and this is the true test.

On the other hand, love does not respond this way. The person in love is focused on the one they love, not themselves. They have an understanding that because their partner loves them, their needs will continually be a priority for their partner.

You may think that love is a two-way street, but just like lust, it is a one-way street. The difference is in the direction of the street. Lust is directed towards selfishness and love is directed to selflessness.

There is a huge difference between love and lust in that lust fulfills a selfish pleasure or desire that can vary to a great degree. Love fulfills the desire and pleasure of another, not-self. That's why you can love someone who does not love you. That's why you can love someone who does not even love themselves.

Yes, lust and love are both one-way streets that are heading in opposite directions. Lust focuses on self and self-gratification, but love focuses on others and their satisfaction. Love is the single most powerful force in the universe.

A healthy relationship is a two-way street because both partners love each other selflessly. Their focus is on their partner, and they trust that the love they are giving will be returned to them.

You can be an amazing superhero and an amazing man that has incredible skill, money, good looks, and body build, but without love, you are absolutely nothing. You are an empty shell of a man. Why? Because you were meant to love selflessly.

Many men today are filled with lust and are in lust. They were meant to be filled with love and be in love. Lust is a selfish blood-sucking creature that has little care for its victims.

Lust's purpose always ends in personal pleasure. Deception can occur when you like and lust for someone at the same time. There is the hope of real love growing from this "like", but where the intent is mixed with lust, it will often backfire.

Lust won't stop until it gets what it wants. It uses you up and fills its hunger until it's hungry again and needs to be fed. I know men who think they love women, but they only lust for them. They go from girl to girl to fill a void deep inside themselves. They are looking only to fill their self-pleasure and long to gratify their out-of-control passions.

They have believed the lie that they love women when they just love the idea of women like they love food or cars. They don't love them, they love themselves. They may even like some women but have become the very thing that resists love. They have become a lie. They may have multiple girlfriends, gaining what they want from each of them, but never loving any of them.

The song from Wanda Mallette, Bob Morrison, and Patti Ryan with the lyrics *"looking for love in too many faces"* and *"looking for love in all the wrong places"* comes to mind. This is an interesting song that many believe, though it portrays a misconception and a lie. You don't go looking for love.

When you're "looking" for something you're hoping to "find" something. This longing to find something is not love, but a filling of selfishness and lust. That does not mean that someone can't have a true desire to be loved. It means that love finds you, you can't find love.

Most people who fall in love fall in love over time. Something happens as they focus on the other person and not themselves. As their attention is on another and not themselves, they discover how much they care for and like this person.

There, "like" gradually evolves to "love" and all they want to do is to make the other person happy. They don't care about the cost or the price they must pay, only that the person they love is happy. I'm not referring to money or a financial price to pay. I'm referring to the cost of what you may have to give up for a relationship with her; for her to be the only one in your life. This is the price you will pay for your decision and commitment to her alone.

You may be thinking, "how do I find the person that may love me?" Or "if I am not searching for love, then how am I to be found by love?"

People can enjoy each other's company in many ways. Having fun, noticing things about someone you like, and a desire to be with someone are all very natural ways of forming relationships.

It is not lusting to enjoy and like another person's company. There is a sharing going on back and forth which often happens among developing friendships. It's normal to want to be around someone you begin to care for. The more you care, and the more time you spend together, will reveal what's next. Lust, like, love, or maybe just good friends.

So how can you tell if you love someone? How can a man use this superpower? Understanding what defines perfect love will be vital to having proper behavior that flows from true love.

Let's look at what perfect love is and what it is not. The things love does and does not do.

Love does not burst out in anger too quickly. You will get mad at times but won't burst out angrily at the one you love. Love does not look to get even for something done to them but quickly lets it go. Having a quick temper and losing self-control is not an expression of perfect love.

Love gives others the benefit of doubt and does not over-react in situations. Love patiently waits without responding too fast. Love is willing to allow others the grace to be human without jumping to conclusions. Being gentle with others is an expression of love, as well as being gentle with your words and your actions.

This does not mean you won't make mistakes or say things you wish you didn't. I know many men, me included, who wish they can take back some things said. None of us show perfect love, but it should be our aim. The quote from Alexander Pope comes to mind: "to err is human, to forgive is divine."

Keep in mind love grows over time. Someone doesn't immediately have full love. They have a form of love that can increase and grow with time. If it can increase it can also decrease, just like a bank account. The more positive acts of love you put in your account, the more it will grow. The more negative things you say or do will take out withdrawals.

Unfortunately, many men are living in relationships that have severely negative balances. Men misunderstand that one positive word or action adds slowly to the love account, but one negative word or action subtracts rather quickly from the account of love. I know that does not seem fair, but it's life.

I've heard it said that it takes seven positive words to heal the wound caused by one negative word. If you're in the hole and have a negative balance, don't give up!

Don't think that you can fix it too quickly, either. Time can heal most wounds with positive actions, words, and choices. It takes time and acceptance. Some people will never let go of things done or said to them. They are stuck and there is nothing you can do. They must do it for themselves. You can't force them to accept you or your apology because love does not control others.

If you can force someone to love you and do what you want, then that's not true love. That's slavery. In a loving healthy relationship, there is always freedom of choice and respect for what is chosen. Even if you don't agree with the choice someone makes, you must respect their decision. They are not robots or servants.

The risk here, that will always be present in a healthy relationship, is the risk of someone making a wrong choice. People can make some good and some bad choices. You must have faith that they will choose well.

In a healthy loving relationship, good decisions will be made for mutual benefit. But it does not always work that way. A broken image and believing lies can lead some people to choose some pretty bad things.

You may feel like you need to step in and stop someone from making a certain choice, but you can't. You can offer some advice that may help, but you can't stop their decision. Some life-threatening choices may demand that you act, and you must, but eventually for them to grow, they must learn to choose well for themselves.

Love that does not control, but allows others to choose, does not discriminate. Having the right to make a choice does not mean your choice is acceptable. It is merely your choice, and the results are yours to endure. When your decision affects others, they also have the right to choose what is best. You may not like the battle of conflicting choices but that is life.

Choice can be right or wrong, but it is a choice. You can't force someone to love you, it's their choice. The choices we make bring us closer or farther apart.

Your love for someone cannot be so extremely fixed on her acting a certain way or doing certain things, that it removes her freedom.

Love requires flexibility within a relationship to make choices and to be free, even if the choices are wrong. Likewise, the other party does not have to agree with or always accept your choices. They do, however, have to respect your decision.

The consequences of our choices are what we all must live with, no matter who we are. Love does not demand the attention of others. It's not just about you anymore. A relationship consists of more than one person.

When you constantly brag about what you have done and what you have achieved, you tend to forget about your plus one. It's not about what you achieved alone but what you've accomplished together. Don't be that person who must always show off what they have done.

In a healthy relationship, the other person will often let you know when you did a good job. Your focus is not on collecting personal trophies, but on celebrating the trophies of those you love. There is a synergy in a healthy relationship, working together for mutual benefit. Each is focused on the other, not themselves.

Like two people on a teeter-totter, for a relationship to work well, both must work together and for the other person. Love is not there to build self. Love builds others. It wants to see others increase and grow. Love does not concentrate on personal edification and inflating of ego. Love cares for others and wants what is best for them.

When you're in love with someone, you don't act in a way that would disrespect the person you love. Love acts in a way that always shows respect. Men can show small acts of respect that help them to reinforce greater respect. Like opening a door, doing dishes, helping with laundry, and even writing a small note. These little things that she may like reminds her of her value and your respect for her.

It's not important for the person who loves to always be right. Having all the details arranged perfectly for you to be right may work in a courtroom, but not in relationships. Being right is not the primary concern - being together is. You must be more willing to be wrong than to be divided.

A primary concern is not in winning a disagreement, but how to work this out amicably. There is an understanding that for one person to win that another person must lose. That's not togetherness, but division. For them both to win, they must win together as one unit.

Love does not purposely use words to verbally cut another person emotionally. It's not about stirring up their feelings to get them to act out or respond. Edging someone on until they blow up is not an act of love. Purposefully making someone angry does not reflect their best interest.

When two people are in love, they don't keep track of the little mistakes that often are made in life. Instead, they learn from them and try to not repeat them. Love does not hold little things over the head of the one they love. They forgive and let it go without constantly bringing it back up.

When you continually remind someone of their wrongs and the things they did in the past, you are telling them you can't get over what they did. You are stuck there. Though you may have previously agreed to move on, it was a lie.

When you hold grudges, you are secretly telling them that you expect them to be perfect and they cannot make mistakes. It's another form of secret control to pull the metaphorical rug out from underneath them. You try to position yourself in control to win, but you are losing, and losing a lot.

Your lie will sever ties of love because true love forgives. It does not keep track of past mistakes but is present and future minded.

Now if the other person keeps repeating negative actions, that is a different matter altogether.

When you're building something together, there are times in life where the elements of life continually pound down on you causing something to break or rot. This is like a wooden porch where dry rot may appear. Removing the rot and replacing it is probably best and will save the porch from being completely removed. If you neglect to repair the little rot, then you may find yourself down the road years later without a porch.

Dealing with and removing little things in a relationship without letting them build-up will help keep your relationships healthier and better protected against complete failure.

Love does not like to see people mistreated. Injustice and innocent people being hurt directly irritates someone who loves others. They want to help and protect the innocent. A person who loves cannot stand by while unjust actions are being done. They will do what they see as necessary to stop them.

People who love, love the truth. Lies undermine everything we hope to build. Trust is violated by lies. Truth and sincerity keep relationships together. Genuine honesty paves the way for a smoother future together. Sometimes you just need to tell it like it is.

Love is straightforward. It does not try to hide things from others. Keeping secrets is like injecting poison without an antidote. Something may die and it's not worth the risk.

Love is an umbrella that another puts over you to protect you from the rain of life. They believe in you and always build your confidence. They keep you away from things that can hurt or harm you. Love expects the best for you and stands behind you while waiting for the best to come. It holds you up when life's pressure wants to push you back.

Love helps you to achieve your highest potential in life. It won't ever fail you! What great power there is in love. It's what is needed most in our lives and the world.

True love may seem, as described above, out of reach to many. You may look at your life and think you're just too far from love. You may even think that it is just too hard to love like that. Remember love grows. If your aim is true love, it will grow. If you have just a little of what was described as true love two things will happen. First, you will be happy with what you have. Secondly, you will want more.

When men realize what love truly is, they can begin to use this ability of theirs to become their best. To have the best relationships. To treat others the way they deserve to be treated. To be what others deserve for them to be. To be someone's superhero.

Developing Your Superpowers

Having the power of justice, dependability, peace, fun, self-control, and love empower a man to be the best superhero there ever was. When a man is at his best, he possesses all the necessary traits to improve the lives of those around him. But how do you develop these superpowers?

Superpowers for men are developed over time. As men learn to increase their skills through practice with each challenge, their character improves. The actions they take during these challenges will be the true test of their transformation. Each character trait developed will be continuously put to the test through trials.

Changing into a superhero won't happen overnight. Even though it will be difficult in the beginning, consistent actions that show improvements in character will become more and more routine. Eventually, you will become a changed man.

Whether it's his spouse, his children, or a friendly neighbor, a man is there to help the people in his life as needed. Investing in these relationships isn't about himself or what these people can do for him. He is always thinking of ways he can make a difference in their lives.

Sometimes just his mere presence is all that is required. Other times, people may need a helping hand. Maybe something encouraging or positive is all that needs to be heard. He often can cheer up their day by having some fun. Sometimes someone just needs to be held.

Mastering these powers, when needed most, takes time and effort. Improvement comes from use and practice. Knowing when to be a man of peace and when you need to stand against injustice develops as you listen to what is important.

When children know they are loved, the more secure they will feel. The same applies to your entire family. The more love you show them creates an environment where they feel safe and secure. When they know without a doubt that you love them, they begin to flourish. This also helps them overcome life's challenges when they come.

Balancing fun activities with your children, while being the most reliable person your wife knows, also offers security and safety. They can count on you and will always enjoy their time with you.

This balancing act, which continuously needs to occur, can't be accomplished when you are out of sync and not using all your superpowers.

All men have these superpowers, but it's up to them to develop them. Many men have these superpowers buried under a fragmented image, a life of lies, and living as a villain.

Don't Be a Villain

The villain is the man who refuses to change and grow and does not allow "true" character to be formed in his life. He is the man who is living his life with his character misaligned.

This is like driving a car with its alignment off. The car will constantly pull you in the wrong direction. Growing up, my father owned an orange Ford Bronco truck. You could easily see it coming from quite a distance away. He loved (liked) this vehicle. It wasn't in great shape, but with some minor repairs, it seemed to do the job.

It wasn't until I turned sixteen and acquired my permit that I understood what being out of alignment meant. The Bronco's steering wheel was not properly aligned. It had about a three-inch gap where there was no turning control.

This proved to be more hazardous than I originally thought, especially when driving fast. Around town with a thirty mile an hour speed limit was easily manageable. Going on the highway at fifty-five to sixty miles per hour was completely different.

The speed, combined with this issue, and the needed reaction time, made it difficult to stay straight in my lane. My father had made it look so easy as he had grown accustomed to it. He preferred it to the cost of getting it fixed.

I'm still confused about how he managed to hold a cigar in one hand, a coffee in the other, and drive around using his knees.

Many men are like my father in this regard. They would rather stay with their out-of-aligned image than pay the cost to change. Some men get comfortable with their alignment off and pretend their stubbornness and immaturity is macho. To them, the discomfort they face by making real change is worse than the negative impact their villainous actions have on others.

They don't care how it impacts others around them. They like their comfort more. It's what they are used to. They are living with a fragmented image, and they don't seem to mind.

How big is the gap in your alignment? What are you accepting as normal behavior that needs alignment? Real men don't live with these gaps that hurt others.

Some men have accepted a lie, and personally redefined what they think "man" is. They live for themselves. Their vision is small. The impact their life has on others is minimalized by themselves. They are content to live as the villain.

Men often rush around in life taking no thought as to who and how they are hurting others. Like this heavy Ford Bronco truck, they don't realize the impact of their strength on others.

Shortly after I received my driver's license, my sister bought a car. It was used, but new to her, a Chevy Nova.

One night, she parked her car behind my father's Bronco. She had to leave early the next day and didn't want to bother anyone to move his truck.

The thing is, she didn't tell anyone, and my father permitted me to use his Bronco to see my girlfriend (who became my wife years later). I was so focused and determined to get there fast that I never noticed the Nova that was parked right behind the Bronco.

The Bronco was so powerful and strong I never realized I was pushing her Nova backward into a deep ditch along our driveway. I was in such a hurry and was behind a lot of strength, and I didn't notice until her car was completely in the ditch.

This is common for men. They don't know the strength they have. If not balanced and used for good, it can be destructive while rushing around their life selfishly.

A man who refuses to accept his superhero powers to help others is living as a villain. He is limiting himself and his positive impact on others at the same time. By limiting his good character, he is multiplying his bad.

Not accepting your superpowers as a man does not take away your powers, it just reverses them and makes you the villain. Your absence hurts those who are depending on you. Your lust is decaying the love you have for others.

Selfish men only care for their wants and neglect the needs of others. They act like boys who create chaos, rather than being men of peace. These men try controlling others because they cannot control themselves. Rather than defending injustice, they are committing acts of injustice and hurting the innocent people they were meant to protect.

You can be better!

You are a hero yet undiscovered. A diamond in the rough. A lie looking for exposure to the truth. A boy that can be a man.

It's your choice. You have the choice to be the villain or to be the hero. There is nothing in between.

You must be willing to change and to make the necessary corrections to be super. Change your thinking, begin to feel, don't limit yourself, and do what you were meant to do.

Be a man! Be a superhero. Even if you have not mastered all these skills, that's alright. Use the ones you have while working to develop the others. You'll be glad you did and so will your loved ones.

Questions for Self-Reflection

How would you describe your character?

How has your father positively and negatively impacted what you have become?

What is your superpower? How do you use it to help others?

What superpowers do you need to develop? Why?

How can you combine and balance your superpowers to have a greater impact?

6

A Lack of Courage

Men today face many challenges that want to hold them back from their full potential. Despite many environmental and social factors, the biggest challenges men face lays deep within themselves.

Looking deep within a man can be a scary undertaking and many men will do just about anything to avoid it, like lying.

About 10 years ago, I purchased a brand-new vehicle. I was so pumped. I worked hard and achieved something nice. It may not have been the nicest and newest model the dealer had, but I liked it.

We were able to trade in a couple of our other vehicles and drive away with a new Subaru Tribeca. It had electric seats that were very comfortable, a modern-looking navigation system, sunroof, and a tremendously smooth ride.

I was very happy. Much to my surprise, and my total embarrassment, two weeks after owning the vehicle my wife asked me a simple question: "Sam, have you looked under the hood yet?"

After a long silence from me and a laugh from her, my secret was exposed. No, I had not. I had not even considered looking under the hood, and why? The vehicle was running perfectly. I didn't even think of it. (This was years before I had worked doing minor mechanics.)

Today's man is no different. Looking under the hood when you think everything is fine makes no sense. At least when it comes to men looking deep inside themselves.

For most men, looking under the hood of the car may have been the first thing they did. Not me. In our family, my wife grew up in the car business and I just liked driving.

Most men would take better care of their cars than their psychological self. Why? There is safety and security in that which is physical - that which can be seen, touched and is mechanical.

When it comes to issues of the heart, mind, emotions, relationships, and actions, it's more hidden and more difficult to understand. It can be quite scary.

It has always been interesting to me that men would love to get their hands dirty while fixing something that was broken - as long as that something is not themselves.

The external things they can see and feel provide a safe fix. They are more easily defined by clearer rules that are more consistent to follow.

A mechanic can diagnose a car and then proceed to fix it exactly how it's meant to be done. He cannot change how to fix something or to change where the part needs to go. Parts go specifically in a certain way. It's predictable if you know the car. If he fails to follow the instructions, the vehicle may not operate correctly. This made it easy for me to be a mechanic and replace parts. I didn't need to know the relationship from one part to another or know answers to all the why's. That's what the other more seasoned mechanics were there for.

Relationships are not as easily defined. They don't come with a clear and concise set of rules that are easily fixable. This makes them very unpredictable. To a man, it can be intimidating and scary, though he may not admit that.

In his relationships, he struggles to find safety and security in what he cannot see and fix manually. Oftentimes, he will try to force a fix as if it's a mechanical solution, just to make things work. He doesn't understand why it doesn't work. Dads often try to be Mr. Fix it and come up with solutions rather than just listening. No answers are required sometimes.

We have heard it said before that children don't come with instructions, neither do women! Relationships are much more complex than a simple machine. They involve emotions, thoughts, and actions that are constantly evolving.

People just don't stay the same. They are ever-changing and never stay still. They can be predictable and extremely unpredictable at the same time.

Several factors are out of our control. We may think we have all the right tools to handle each situation, but the complexity of the human psyche is too great.

The best way for a man to begin understanding relationships starts with lifting his hood and understanding himself and the complexity of his own engine. He needs to know many things about the engine inside him (the heart). What type of oil does he use? What are the required maintenance and repairs needed?

He needs to ask himself, "Who am I?" "How do I feel?" "What

do I believe?" "Why am I reacting this way?" "How do I see myself and why?"

This is a starting point where men cannot be afraid to ask these questions. He may discover that by letting go of fear, he can find the faith to be the man he was meant to be, the father his family has been waiting for, the husband that she dreams of, or the person society needs from him.

He can become a courageous man, a man not afraid of the difficult places, a man who is willing to stand, and a high-powered one-of-a-kind dream car that has been completely rebuilt.

A Weapon of Mass Destruction

Fear is a weapon that can destroy your life like no other. It sets limits on you that will cause you to self-destruct. You were not meant to live in fear. You were not meant to be a coward or be held back.

One of the fears that can plague your life is the fear of failure. This fear can cause you to miss stepping into the opportunities that are right in front of you in life. It holds you back and keeps you from succeeding.

Fear can infect your mindset. You begin to continuously expect bad things to happen and nothing to ever work out. Your fear has become destructive and is keeping you away from taking the necessary actions to move you into your future.

One of the scariest events in my life was when I asked my

wife to marry me. At that time, I could not see any reason she would want to be with me, but I had several reasons to be with her. It was a battle of destiny over my life.

Fear was like a giant in my way, making it a difficult situation. I had to confront the fear head-on, and I was not sure I could do it. It felt as if I was jumping off a cliff without a parachute, in total faith, and feeling extremely vulnerable. I had a glimpse of hope that I would not be rejected.

Fear gripped me. It wanted to stop me and hold me back from asking her "the" question. I didn't even know what a good marriage consisted of. I spent years watching my parents get farther and farther apart.

With nothing to model except imminent failure, I didn't know what outcome to expect. Nothing else in life seemed to be working out for me, but I mustered the courage to jump. It was the best decision I ever made.

Today, I can't imagine life without her. That one triumph over fear changed my future forever. Fear of failure wanted to stop me from getting something good in my life.

What is failure anyway? Over the years I have redefined it through trial and error. I used to believe, and many still believe this way, that failure means to lose at something. That's not a failure, that's just life. In life, we win some things and lose some things.

Life brings us a load of losing and winning battles. Sometimes we seem to lose more often than we win. We may keep expecting that cycle and negative trend to continue. You may even allow yourself to develop a fear that stops you before you even try for anything good.

Losing is looming at us like a self-proclaimed prophecy.

But failure is not losing! Losing at something is how we learn. Losing is how we grow. It's part of the process in life.

What exactly is being a failure, then? Failure is being knocked down and refusing to get back up. Failure is staying down after losing. It's refusing to get back up and refusing to change and grow. It's losing at something and letting that loss hold you back from ever trying again.

Fear comes in to tell you you're done - finished. Fear says, "It didn't work out last time and if you do it again it still won't work out."

This type of fear is not just believing it won't work next time, but that it will never work for you. Fear keeps you from trying again and failure is now born.

Fear reminds me of smoke. It clouds the real issue so that you don't see clearly. Fear makes you think there is an impassable wall in front of you when it's just "smoke and mirrors."

Fear, while it feels real, pretends to be a barrier that is impossible to conquer. As you begin to see fear as a fake barrier of smoke, you realize it is possible to conquer, and then you can muster the courage to walk through it.

As you break through these pretend barriers presented to you by fear, you will walk into possible opportunities. Don't misunderstand me on this. These barriers are not real, but they feel very real. It's like a bad dream after you have been awakened. It seems so real, but now that you're awake you realize your fear was built on false facts. The feelings of fear are real but the evidence often that led to fear is lacking.

It's time to wake up to reality and away from fear. Opportunities are waiting for you to wake up to them. Some will work and some will not work, but you will grow and learn along the way.

Remember the saying, "better to have tried and failed than to never have tried at all". It really should say, "better to have tried and learned from it, then to never have tried at all."

When we believe the lie that not winning is a failure, then we lose the opportunity to learn from a loss. We become obsessed with the mindset that winning is always "success." When it becomes the only way for us, then we never allow ourselves to lose, and we never learn.

With this mindset, we will do anything to win and ensure that I'm not in second place or worse. I must be first, I must win! We become either ultra-competitive or we just give up. There seems to be nothing in between.

As I am writing this, I am thinking about how many schools have adopted rules in sports where everyone wins. We are all winners. No losers. That's just not real life. These schools have a false view of what it means to lose at something.

Losing does not mean I am a failure. It means I did not win this time. I guess that the reason they have adopted this perspective is in response to how losing makes one feel. I can understand this side of it. To see a child sad from losing a game is hard for anyone to deal with. It can break your heart to see them so sad. Is the answer to make them all pretend to be winners?

These schools necessarily are not to blame. They have taken on the lie that we as men have believed. This lie is that when we lose, we are a failure. Fear keeps us trapped in this lie, so we won't progress and grow. The issue with teaching children that they are all winners, and no one loses, is we are teaching them to live a lie.

When you cannot lose you cannot learn. Why try? Why advance? Give me an A+ just for showing up to class! Avoiding the truth because we don't want to deal with sad feelings and negative emotions is not the answer.

By making everyone a winner, we are coaching everyone to fail. Fail in school, fail in the workplace, and fail in life. Why try? Why learn? Why grow? I am a winner just as I am.

Letting everyone win is a cop-out. It's a simple response to a deeper issue. Encouraging children through their loss, that they are not a loser, helps them to manage and learn to cope with their negative emotions. It also helps children to begin to learn how to grieve properly, and not be overcome by loss. If children are unprepared, this type of loss can be devastating. No one wants a child to experience loss, especially the death of a loved one. Helping them cope effectively with other smaller types of losses will begin to prepare them for the bigger ones in life. They will learn that no matter how painful it is and no matter the loss, that eventually they must get back up and continue with their life. They learn to move forward taking the memories of the loss and loved one with them rather than letting it forever crush them.

When children lose at something, this does not mean they are losers based on how they performed. Their value is not in their performance, it is in who they are individually.

The things we do in life don't define who we are, we do. It's defined by who we are inside. How we handle losing. How we handle winning. How we treat others. How we get back up and keep going.

How we grow and learn from our past behaviors can make us better people inside. We learn that whatever we do, whether we win or lose, we truly win by our attitude, character, and trying again.

Not everyone can be first. Not everyone is a super athlete. Even someone who wins outwardly can be an internal loser. Life is not defined on the football field, soccer field, or basketball court. It's decided before and after each game, in practice and at home. Who we are at these in-between places is who you are.

Only after we have learned to deal with the positive and negative feelings associated with winning and losing can we truly appreciate how difficult it is to win at something. We appreciate the effort and applaud the success, as well as admire the hard work and growth needed to get there.

Everyone likes to win, but not everyone has what it takes to be a real winner - inside and out. Not all people can be an external winner, like at a sport, but everyone can be an internal winner.

Men have for so long tried to identify their success by what they do outwardly. They believe in a lie that their job or performance makes them better than others. They are afraid to admit it's a cover-up or magic trick.

This lie tells you that if people focus on what I am doing well, then maybe they won't see who I am inside, and how I feel about myself and my life.

This is the ultimate sleight-of-hand, a con artist that some have come to admire. Shallow and fearful men isolated by work, status, and performance, are afraid to admit who they "really" are. They are afraid to lose, so they never learn and never truly win.

Through fear, these men believe the lie that performance and jobs define them. They think this is who they are.

They are blinded by smoke and mirrors and lack the courage to stand up and walk forward. They need the courage to look within and be willing to change. They need to realize that it's not what they do that makes them a real man, but who they are.

Your performance on the field or at work may give you temporary applause, but it's the man you are inside that will make it last lifelong. Don't let the fear of failure become the weapon that destroys who you were meant to be.

Never Too Close

Fear can seem as dangerous as some natural disasters, and unfortunately, we often are content to just live with it.

Hawaii is beautiful, and people who live there live with the risk of an occasional volcanic eruption. People know the risk and can avoid being hurt by adhering to warnings. They may still have to face the reality of property damage and loss, but by listening to evacuation warnings, they can save their lives.

Personal fear, in comparison, can be much worse. It's not something you can live with and then just get away from when life begins to erupt all around you. It stays with you until you confront it. Often, there are very few warnings until you're consumed by it.

Left unconfronted, fear will limit your potential and keep you from experiencing a full and meaningful life. You can't get away from it until you confront it head-on. It's like taking the danger of a volcano with you wherever you go, without escaping. This won't change until you confront it!

This may seem like a drastic example, but many men would rather live with fear than confront it. Unfortunately, living in fear devastates a man's life, hindering it in all aspects. Just like a volcano's lava covers everything in its path, fear has no boundaries in one's life, when it is given the power to flow.

The resulting devastation from fear can severely hurt relationships in a man's life, that was meant to be lived free of fear.

Many men do not like to feel certain emotions. It makes them feel weak. This is a fear of intimacy. This is not a fear of sex. It's a fear of someone seeing who you are inside and having to share that with them. They see who you are, and you see who they are.

I have heard it said that intimacy means, "into me you see." Women seem to have a natural inclination towards this type of proximity. For a man, it just feels uncomfortable.

The more a man defines his strength by physical attributes, the more he may resist his emotional attributes. He perceives his strength from his physique or his intellect, rather than his emotional intelligence.

Fear tells him that feeling certain emotions makes him weak. Sharing openly in a relationship leads to feeling vulnerable, which only reinforces his insecurity that he is weak. This reasoning is just not true. It's a lie many men have believed.

The feeling of being uncomfortable is a true feeling that is felt. It's something new and is uncharted territory. That's what makes it feel so uncomfortable. It's normal to feel uneasy about something new.

It's also easier to believe, because women are so good at this, that it's just a woman thing. That's not true either. This thinking promotes the lie that women are not strong, but weak.

Biologically, most men are physically stronger than women, but strength is not defined by mere biology. Women can have the character, intellect, and passion that displays fortitude stronger than many men.

There is an extra strength that comes from combining the attributes you feel comfortable with and adding new ones that feel uncomfortable.

When you push through the fear and awkwardness, you begin to practice a new skill set that will make you ultimately stronger. It will take some time and practice, but you will learn how to be more open in a way that brings you closer to those you love.

With practice, it will become more comfortable, and after a while, you will begin to realize how feeling emotions and expressing yourself appropriately with your spouse makes you stronger, not weaker.

I think it's important to mention that some males have embraced emotions as their only strength or their primary strength. This is not what I am talking about. Many men fear that if they become more intimate, they will lose their manhood. Believe me, if you fear that, then you have nothing to worry about.

A man that is always about emotions is out of balance. So is a man that is all about physical strength. This is not about giving up your manhood; it's about embracing what manhood truly stands for.

Manhood is not trying to be like a woman. It's being a man who understands when to be tough and when to be sensitive.

It's knowing when and how to "open up" emotionally with those close to you - not every other person on the planet.

It's showing the ones you love that not only are you physically or mentally strong, but you also have a big heart and love them too. You're willing to go beyond just showing them how much you love them - you're willing to tell them.

People close to us need to hear things. Deep trust is built by hearing how much you care. Those closest to you need to continually be reassured that you care for them.

When your children are facing things that are difficult to understand and hard to experience, they need to hear from you. When your wife is feeling overwhelmed and unsettled, she needs to hear from you.

Don't let fear keep you from your finest moments. Fear says, don't do it, stay tough! But your rigidness will bruise, scar, and close them off to you.

Your gentleness and openness in these moments will create a bond and a closeness that they will always remember. Sometimes just being present is enough. Other times they need you to be there and to share.

Don't allow the fear of intimacy to intimidate you from being the best version of yourself you can be. Reach down and gather some "really" powerful and sensitive strength.

This kind of strength requires you to face some things that are uncomfortable and awkward. This power within you will make you a better father, husband, and leader.

The ability to overcome fear and embrace a new "you" is found from the courage within.

The Power of Fear

I'm not sure what was going on in my life that attracted such fear, such evil. I'm not sure I'm the one to blame. What we desire and what we think often draw forces to us like a magnet.

I heard stories about my grandfather's association with the mob, but I never really saw that side of him in action. I only knew that I was named after him for a reason. What that reason was I didn't know, and my imagination filled in the gaps.

It's not unusual for an adolescent to admire someone in a position of power. And that's exactly what I did. I so admired my grandfather and I wanted to be just like this man I hardly knew.

I was devastated at age eight when I got the news that he passed away from a heart attack while sleeping. I felt my very existence and purpose being snatched away from me. I was lost in a deep black hole without escape.

Meanwhile, my parents asked me to choose who I wanted to live with: mom or dad, you chose. This dark hole seemed black enough. It now added new feelings of confusion and feeling all alone. I refused to decide, this was not my decision to make.

The grief and the confusion, combined with hate towards my father, all culminated in an uncontrollable rage. I would often punch holes in the walls, tease others, and set things on fire. Something inside me wanted others to feel the pain that I was feeling deep inside.

A BB gun, slingshot, and my fists found innocent targets any-where I could bring destruction. I would shoot at any moving target, and I am lucky that I didn't poke my eye out.

Yes, it was my idea for some friends and me to take our BB guns to the cemetery and shoot at each other for fun. When that proved to be too painful physically, I turned to my slingshot. I wanted to be able to hit everything and anything.

My aim was terrible. Until, to my surprise, I hit a bird in a tree. The horrible feelings I had inside and seeing that beautiful bird lying there dead made me give up my slingshot for good.

That incident also pulled on how I was feeling inside. Secretly, I was afraid that I would be all alone. I felt dead. I was afraid of my future and felt powerless to do anything about it.

This fear seemed to grow and express itself randomly. It became the night thief that robbed me of having a peaceful sleep.

Life seemed bleak and I was offered no real reason to live. It's no wonder why I started having suicidal nightmares that no one knew about. Something about this fear deep inside me was attracting some real dark powers.

I remember trying to climb in bed with my mom for safety but could not escape the torturous feeling of falling deeper into this black hole. Darkness was pulling me in deeper now. For months this would go on and on and seemed to be increasing in intensity.

The random dream that started as an adventure, walking downtown, would ultimately culminate in jumping off a bridge, ending my life. This dream would not stop, it would not end. It became the only dream I would have every night, night after night, for weeks upon weeks.

I would do anything to have a peaceful sleep, but it seemed

impossible. Sleep was now my enemy, my greatest fear. I had to face this fear every night as my body eventually resisted all attempts to stay conscious.

I don't remember much of anything else. School and the rest of life was a blur. All my effort and strength went into resisting my ultimate fear - death.

One Saturday night I managed to fight sleeping for quite a while. The lie that I felt sick helped to lessen my parent's agitation with my insomnia. My bedroom door opened and closed, and to my surprise, a doctor was standing there. He came over to my bed, kneeling to measure my temperature, pulse, and respiration. I didn't know this person, but he came with credentials and a white doctor's coat. I thought that my parents sent him in to check on me.

I had no idea the evil he represented, and nothing could have prepared me for what he did next. Startling me, he glared into my eyes and said these words, "And you know the dreams you've been having? You will hit the water in your dream and never wake up."

Then, he left my room with me shaking in a state of frozenness and utter fear. Shaking and frozen, I could not speak. I was trying to scream for help, but I just laid there helplessly trembling in fear until I eventually passed out.

I have never experienced anything like that before. What could that have been? Who was it? How did he know what I told no one? What kind of power was this? That night I woke up again from my dream after jumping from the bridge before hitting the water.

Something was trying to lure me in with my fear and take my

life away. I had no clue what it could be. It seemed so powerful and scary to me.

My parents never sent anyone in to see me. Was this real? Was this a psychological episode or a dream? I don't know. I was the only witness to these facts and the fear I felt.

That Sunday morning, I was invited by a friend to attend a church service. I had never been to a church before, so I went out of curiosity. I don't remember much about the service, except the minister saying that God can be my father and I can be his child. I thought to myself that I could use a father.

This Jesus they said rose from the dead. Wow, that is "real" power. I went to the altar and prayed for the first time in my life. I felt different, I felt free. I had a desire to discover more about this power and this person, Jesus.

That night, I had the best sleep I have had in months. I never had that nightmare again. Something was now different, I was different.

The fear that seemed to constantly control me daily, from within me now was manageable. Somehow, I now had peace from this storm. Fear found a worthier opponent in me - faith. As faith grew in me, my fear would decrease.

The light I discovered was more powerful than any form of darkness. I was living proof. Now my dream of being in the mafia had vanished, I knew that I was made for so much more. I would have to overcome other outward battles of fear, but they were no match for my faith.

I had new courage and a new strength to fight that I never had before.

True Strength

Courage is having true strength. It's the ability to face something that may be frightening or scary.

Men today need more courage. It's no wonder that most men have traded real courage for liquid courage. Rather than having an endless supply of courage within, they would rather drink from a bottle for temporary relief. That is fake courage. It's not the real deal. The courage that comes from being inebriated also comes with poor judgment: the inability to act responsively and gauge what's going on. This is the exact opposite of what your family needs from you.

When someone is under the influence, they may appear more courageous, but they will violate social cues, forget gentleness, and can't balance their abilities effectively. They become the very weakness they often fear when sober.

Their friends and family are left having to deal with situations alone while they are oblivious to what is happening.

Courage comes from the word in another language for "heart." It means to "have heart." It combines your feelings with a sound state of mind fit for appropriate action. Emotions, unhinged from a stable frame of mind, bring chaos and disorder.

Men should have the courage to embrace passionate action using their full aptitudes. Your family deserves it. They don't deserve the insensitive, abusive, distant, or degrading male that comes with drinking spirits.

True courage faces life and its challenges with the best of who you are. Courage is a trait highly admired. We see this in movies and the stories that are often told.

From a cowardly lion that finds his courage to the brave battles fought for a higher purpose, we are always looking for "a few good men." You can be that man.

Courage to face our fears comes in many forms. Courage shows up when you take that first step asking her to marry you, taking a risk. If she says no, what will you do? If she says yes, how will it all play out?

When you hold your child for the first time, determined to protect him/her from harm, not knowing the full scope of what life will bring, that takes courage.

Going to work, paying the bills, raising children, being with your spouse, being active in your family's life, and being so much more than this, will take courage, and lots of it!

In the good times and the hard ones, in the happy times and the sad, your courage is needed. This courage can be a shoulder for the family to cry on, the tenacity to tackle some hard decisions, soft words of adoration given at the right moment, or a helping hand when you're tired.

You need the willingness to tackle difficult challenges in ways that are best for your loved ones. Sometimes, you will need to be tough but not rough. You will have to be gentle, but not fragile. You will need to be willing to "open up", not "close up." Face things don't walk away.

Courage is knowing when to stand up and support someone or to sit down and encourage them. We need to know when to be alert and when to sleep. Courage steps up but doesn't show off. It lifts others and does not hold them down.

But most of all, you must never, never, never let fear ruin your life or hold you back from being your best.

Twenty Pounds of Courage

One of my wife's relatives owned a farm, but it was not the normal farm that you'd think of. There were no cows and no crops - only turkeys.

Our visit here was fascinating since we had never been to a turkey farm before. We loved hearing about everything turkey.

Growing up, I had a fascination with turkeys. They would gather often around the property where I lived, and I was always looking for an adventure. I remember hiding this long thick rope in my fathers' garage. I would often practice, like a cowboy, lassoing anything I could. I practiced on tree limbs, fence posts, my dog, and even sometimes my brother.

I'm not sure what possessed me that day riding home on the school bus. As the bus came to my home, I couldn't believe my eyes. Dozens of wild turkeys were in the field next to my house.

I was on a mission from the first sighting and nothing was going to stop me. I don't remember the bus stopping or getting off it. All I remember was grabbing that rope and running as fast as I could towards those turkeys.

My goal was to lasso the rope around one of their long necks. That's as far as I thought it through. What I didn't realize was how fast they were. I remember thinking, "how can they run so fast being such big fat birds?"

They ran right across the road and over a big embankment. By the time I could catch up to them, they vanished. I was baffled. Where could they have gone? It never occurred to me to look up in the trees. They were just too big to fly. Right?

These are the types of turkeys I expected to see when we visited the turkey farm, but I was mistaken. The difference between the turkeys we were visiting, and the ones I knew growing up, was significant. The turkeys on this farm were domesticated, and the ones where I lived growing up were wild. These domesticated turkeys seemed more like oversized chickens than turkeys.

I heard stories about these birds. Domesticated turkeys seem to have become a completely different bird. They turn white, they can't fly, their necks and legs are shorter, and they seem to lose their intelligence.

I remember a story told by our relative, the turkey farmer, about how curious domesticated turkeys are. She said that when it rains, the turkeys are so curious about the drops of water hitting their heads that they would continuously look up.

I've been told they can drown this way, but others say that is just folklore. Either way, it appears that when a turkey loses its main purpose and its protective nature, the curiosity gene takes center stage.

Unlike domesticated turkeys, wild turkeys are considered territorial and brave. They are often seen defending their own space without giving up.

A wild turkey can fly almost one mile, and upwards of fifty

miles per hour. It is said that at times they can even outrun a horse. They are strong, courageous, and fearless animals.

President Obama's first pardoned turkey in 2009 was named Courage and sent to live in Disneyland. Later in 2016, the headlines started reporting that "Courage the Turkey" is dead.

"Courage is dead." This seems appropriate for today's modern man. Courage is dead and curiosity has taken over. Men have lost their purpose - a purpose to protect their families and territory from forces meant to harm and destroy them.

Men used to stand taller and have longer necks. They would keep on the lookout for anything that could be a danger to their families. If they had to, they would fly and run to help those they love. Now, they have become tamed and curious. They have lost the will to fight and the courage to stand.

They have allowed the curiosities of culture to emasculate their prime directive. Instead of being fearless, strong, and courageous turkeys, they have become chickens.

I'm glad that I didn't lasso a turkey that day. I'm sure it would have been a lesson in "courage" that I would never have forgotten.

They say ignorance is bliss. I'm sure you would agree that as a kid, not knowing things can spare us from the pain of the truth. But for a man, ignorance is no excuse.

How can we live life in fear while our families are paying the price? We can no longer sit ideally by, afraid to do something significant. It's time to stand up for your children and their security. It's time to run to your wife and protect your intimacy. It's time to courageously live the truth - all twenty pounds worth of it. It's time to trade in being a chicken, to be a courageous turkey.

Questions for Self-Reflection

If you were to look under the hood of your life, what would you find and what repairs would you need?

How has being afraid impacted your life?

Do you struggle with the fear of true intimacy? Explain.

Have you allowed courage to be a part of who you are?

What benefits are there to living courageously rather than being fearful?

7

To Go Faster

Nothing will stop you in your tracks faster than getting caught in a lie. It's no wonder that the answer to this dilemma for many men is to never get caught.

Men often dream of better days that will be better for them and their families. As time goes by, they begin to realize that with every passing day, their dreams seem farther and farther away. The solution: let's speed things up to get there faster. More money, things, a promotion, or a bigger house can all be worthy aspirations. When our desire to get these starts to control us, we refuse to let anything get in the way of obtaining them - even the truth.

The farther we veer from the truth, the harder it is to find our way back. It's like driving a car fast. The faster you drive, the less reaction time you have to maneuver the vehicle. Lies can be used to help us reach our goal and speed up the process, but while we may reach our goal, lies never stop there. The destination that lies bring us to is far from the path that we want in life. They take us places we would never dare to go.

Each lie opens a new door that would have never been accessed without them. These doors bring consequences and when lies open one door, many more doors are automatically opened. You may be able to control the first door, but what follows is out of your control.

People have written books that it's okay to lie your way to the top, and once you've made it, then you can use that success to help others and live with having character. They're dead wrong! By then it's too late. Your life was already poisoned by lies.

To get ahead, a man may think that lying can help him. When the foundation of his life is built on lies, it appears that these lies help him to stand higher and build taller. What he doesn't realize is that his foundation is built on top of an impending sinkhole, waiting to collapse.

You can't build something on a faulty foundation. It may last a while, but eventually, it will crumble and fall. Even good foundations that were built correctly can crash when they do not handle damage in the right way. Just like earthquakes and hurricanes are out of our control causing significant damage to foundations, so are the actions of others and the challenges life brings. The impact on a good structure, if not remedied, can be just as catastrophic as a foundation that was built incorrectly.

Florida, a state that is known for perfect weather and memorable vacations, is also home to the largest sinkhole recorded. The Winter Park Sinkhole of 1981 was nearly three hundred and fifty feet wide and seventy-five feet deep. It swallowed a family home and several cars from a luxury car business. It also took with it two streets, an RV trailer, an Olympic-sized pool, and several trees. All were permanently gone.

Visually, where a sinkhole will emerge is unpredictable. It isn't until you explore under the surface of the ground that you can see the impending damage. In Winter Park, a shift in the limestone was the cause of the sinkhole.

This horrible event is a good example of someone who builds their life on lies. Every lie corrupts the very foundation upon which your structure is built. Deep down, the damage that lies cause is buried beneath, even if you can't see the destruction on the surface. Your lies create the vacuum that will swallow away all your success.

Lies may help you go faster, create shortcuts, and make others believe you're someone different than you are, but remember that eventually, the truth will always come through.

It's amazing how people will often lie as if the end justifies the means. They imagine their lies taking them to the point of promotion, a better relationship, more sales, higher income, and winning. They think that's the end when it's not. No one can see the future and know the end. We can only estimate the expected results from a short distance. What we estimate to be the conclusion, is often only the middle.

Liars can't see the sinkhole forming underneath everything they are building on. You can't see the lawsuits forming from your lies. You can't see how your blind ambition has taken you away from quality time with your family. You can't see that your wife has desperately been searching, longing for something more. You have become blinded by your lies and selfish pursuits. You cannot see what you are becoming or have already become.

Your desire to lie has created an appetite that can never

be satisfied. This appetite for more has latched onto you like a leach, which will suck the life right out of you, and you will never see it coming.

There are no shortcuts. All of us are moving at the speed of life. When we try to go faster than what has been mandated for us, we lose the ability to react properly to what is right in front of us.

Don't believe that lies will help accelerate your progress. They will bring you backward, farther than you ever imagined you would go. The worst part is, you will never see it coming before it's too late.

In this chapter, we will look at several examples of where men have used lies for personal advancement and how that has impacted them, and those around them.

The Businessman

Stan, a middle-aged businessman, owned a brokerage firm that he had built from the ground up. After years of working for others, he decided it was time for him to develop his firm.

After watching investment tycoons take advantage of the market in a way that left many at a disadvantage financially, he was motivated to help people. His mission was to help middle-class families make investments that would help them outperform the market. He concluded that while helping others invest, he could also make a fortune for himself along the way.

Unfortunately, things just seemed to be going too slow for

him. Already almost sixty years old, his goal was to reach over one million dollars in personal income within three years. To achieve this, he started putting his goal above his mission. Worse, he started to believe that reaching his goal was the best way to help others.

Desiring to be ten years ahead of where he was, he started to look at procuring some proprietary investments that yielded higher returns. Justifying the higher risk with the higher returns, he knew he was making decisions based on faulty conclusions, but still pushed forward.

Instead of offering clients an investment that best suited their investment needs and risk tolerance, he convinced many to take chances for higher returns, even if they weren't completely comfortable with it.

With the high return, he was able to persuade many people into putting large amounts of money into these investments. Better yet, his goal to reach his one-million-dollar paycheck was nearly obtainable.

Convinced that this was a sure thing, Stan also made some large personal bets on these same investments. Over the next few years, he became the guru of fame and fortune for many. People were seeing returns in their accounts they couldn't believe. If Stan offered an investment, people would want in.

Greed crept in where there used to be caution. Stan knew that things could not stay this way forever and that the market would eventually adjust. He had overheard some news from the owner of the company holding their proprietary investments, that some policy changes would significantly impact profitability. This would affect the investment significantly. He was the only other person with this knowledge.

Stan found a way to secretly sell off large portions of his interest ahead of this news becoming public. His greedy ambition to get ahead blinded him from his better judgment. The lies he had gently spun, though effective in getting investors, did not reflect the entire picture of truth. He put his interest ahead of others and ended up acting upon insider information.

Too bad Stan could not see the end. He thought he could, but he only saw the middle. He only saw how he and his investors were making money but were blinded to the consequences of his actions.

His income dropped significantly from lawsuits and complaints, and an indictment for insider trading was filed against him. His younger wife, who married him for his money, decided to move on to greener pastures.

The sinkhole of lies in his life was becoming evident and everything was just starting to collapse for Stan.

The Salesman

Steve was a good salesman, at least that's what the numbers continuously showed. He was on the top of the performance list often and would do just about anything to stay there - even lie.

Throughout the many sales positions in the past, he had developed a strategy that included cutting corners, bypassing details, fudging numbers, and ignoring procedures. He was going to make a sale, even if he had to misrepresent what he was selling, and he did.

Many times, people would buy what he was selling just to get rid of him because he was so annoying. He didn't care what anyone thought or who he hurt on his path to his next sale. Cheating was just part of the game for him.

He couldn't keep his word because it often would get in the way of making another sale. He became the epitome of the title "liar" and "used car salesman."

After sneaking his way into getting face time with a business owner, he put on his best performance. He strategically overcame any objections and had an answer for everything, even if that answer was untrue. Twisting facts and figures until they said yes, he told every customer what they wanted to hear to turn it into a sale no matter how uneasy they felt about it.

Another sale, another goal, another bonus, another lie. He couldn't see how all his lies were hurting others and himself. While his initial sales were strong, many of his recurring sales fell through because people were misled. He didn't care as he had already received the initial commissions and bonuses.

Steve's lies would catch up to him until, eventually, he moved on to the next sales position. He lived a lie. He was a liar.

Steve was lonely because his lying isolated him from everyone he cared for. Lying offered him shallow relationships, and he had no currency for building any trust. Women only wanted his money, he was involved in recreational drugs, and his money never stayed in his bank account long.

Unless he starts to accept the truth and slow down, he will always be left alone, feeling empty, and living his life full of regret. In time, trust can be regained, and new positive behaviors accepted. He can make an honest attempt to earn a living while being true to himself and others.

Steve can rebuild. It will take time and hard work, but it can be done. With the right foundation, based on truth, he can build better and higher than before. He just needs to take it slow and steady.

He will have to trade his reputation of lies for truth. It won't be easy and won't happen overnight, but eventually, others will find out who he is. His new pace slowed down in truth, will help him live life with all its benefits. No longer will the fast pace of lies hold him back from what's valuable.

For Steve to no longer see others as pawns to step over and to get to his next goal or paycheck, he will have to embrace the truth that respects others.

The Minister

Pastor Dave seemed to have it all together. He had a beautiful family with three children and a lovely wife. As pastor of a local community church, he earns a good salary, excellent benefits, and housing in a nice area.

When he became pastor of the church it was nearly empty. In just three years, he has been able to draw more people to the church and add additional services each week. Dave is a very charismatic person, and people like him. He offers a message that is relevant culturally and the members of Hope Church have come to trust him sincerely.

Despite the growth of his church and its strong group of committed members, Pastor Dave is not completely happy with his ministry. Deep down, he has a longing for something much bigger and a desire to be a pastor of a megachurch like some of the leaders he idolizes.

While other leaders of the church know about Dave's goals to continue growing the church, what they don't know is that a selfish ambition has become his focus. Overlooking the people, he was called to help, he is obsessed with being popular and famous. He is living a lie.

Lies have slowly found their way into his ministry, replacing the integrity he once had. Dave's decisions are now being made based on how he can draw more people for a bigger platform. His desire to get ahead fast has left him focused on himself more than those he was hired to reach out to in the ministry.

Lying about his true intention is creating a conflict of interest and an occupational hazard. A pastor is meant to serve others, not himself. His selfish ambition is harming those he is meant to help.

Pastor Dave needs to be honest with himself. He needs to ask himself the hard question: "Do I want to be popular or effective?" Someone who is meant to lead others in spiritual things cannot be tied to selfish things.

Unfortunately, due to his position of influence, he puts himself and his family in jeopardy of being hurt by his lies. Everyone in his congregation and community is counting on him to do what is right.

If Dave continues down this path that is filled with lies, deception, and selfishness, he will discover that he will eventually self-destruct.

The Investor

Robert is happily married and has two wonderful children. For nearly twelve years, he worked at a transportation company driving trucks, which provided a nice income for his family.

One day while making a routine delivery, he blew out his knee. In his current condition, he could not drive the truck or deliver the products as needed. After being out of work for over a year from this injury, he was offered a small settlement to start a new career.

Considering his options, he decided to start renovating properties. He had always dreamed of trying to flip houses but never had the available cash.

He bought his first foreclosure at an auction on the city steps. As the highest bidder, Robert paid thirty thousand dollars for a three-bedroom, one bath home. He did most of the work himself and after several months of hard work, he was able to sell the property and make a generous profit.

Robert was thrilled with his success. The amount of time and labor that this process took was significant. This first home took away time with his family. He wanted to find a way to speed things up a bit, increase his profit, and get the work done quicker.

Robert decided to take out a loan to buy five more properties and work on them simultaneously. He hired a crew to help with repairs so it would free up his time to manage renovations and look for more properties.

At first, this seemed like a great idea to earn more money faster, but with Robert spread so thin between the different projects, corners were drastically cut. Workers were not managed well and took advantage of their time and resources.

To save money, Robert bought discount, low-quality materials that didn't last. His only goal was to make the houses appear complete on the surface, but many code violations were overlooked, or simply ignored.

When Robert went to sell these homes, he listed the properties himself and lied to prospective homeowners about having multiple offers on each property, so they would have to move quickly. If they wanted the house, he told them that an all-cash offer with no inspection was sure to beat out the other offers. To further push them to make the purchase, he lied about the quality of material used in these houses and ensured that all the work was up to code.

These lies would be his downfall. Later, many unhappy homeowners ended up suing him. Robert got way in over his head and ruined an honest opportunity for himself. He paid out thousands in attorney fees and settlements, putting a financial and emotional strain on his family that would follow them for years.

Robert allowed his greed and desire to go faster to blind him. He thought the end would justify his means, but never saw the true end. He could only see the true middle. The end was not what he imagined. He thought that lying would advance him, not hurt him. His desire to advance financially led to questionable decisions and behaviors.

The consequences of these decisions and behaviors would now follow him and his family moving forward.

Going faster using lies calculates that you can see the end of your justifying to be true. The actual truth is that no one can see the end of their decisions and choices only somewhere in the middle. The end never justifies the means. It's a total sham. The end is far worse when built on lies. The negative consequences can't be seen from your vantage point of reason. You can only estimate where you will be by what has happened to others before you. Lies will destroy you, but a life built on foundations of truth, prepares you for true success.

Questions for Self-Reflection

How has rushing to get ahead backfired on you?

Have you ever lied to get ahead? What consequences resulted?

What foundational issues have caused a sinkhole in your life?

What kind of foundation would you like to build your life on?

What impact has your father's foundation in life had on you?

8

Faulty Reasoning

We have heard it said that the mind is a terrible thing to waste, and that's true, but in some situations, it's a terrible thing to use.

Men have come up with some of the strangest reasons why they do some of the crazy things they do. Many times, you wonder just what was he thinking?

When I was younger, I did some crazy things. What was going through my mind when I decided to slide down a steep hill on a piece of plywood holding onto an attached rope? Not surprisingly, I finished the ride with multiple internal and external stitches in my knee, and I still have a scar to this day.

I could go on and on about the stupid things I did when I was young, and I am sure you could too. I grew out of these foolish immature stunts as many men do. Of course, some men don't. The immaturity of youthful action causes many to wonder what is going on in their minds.

It's kind of like the commercial where a boy asks the owl "how many licks does it take to get to the center of a Tootsie Pop?" When it comes to why some men do what they do, the world may never know.

There are men who, despite getting older, continue with these immature charades. These men seem to never grow up. They still participate in crazy irrational behaviors.

There are many faulty reasons for why men continue to lie, but their explanations are as faulty as their actions. For years, men have used certain justifications to rationalize their behaviors. They are fraudsters, no matter how sophisticated their attempts at lying become.

In the early nineteen hundreds, many discoveries were being made around the world about early man, yet none were found near Great Britain. Also, for the past fifty years, the scientific community had been in awe of Charles Darwin's new evolutionary theory.

Charles Dawson, a lawyer by education, was an unknown amateur archeologist who wanted to make a name for himself. He also wanted to put England on the map to discover evidence that further supported Darwin's new theory.

This became a reality when Dawson discovered skull fragments, a set of teeth, and primitive tools in Piltdown, United Kingdom. Dawson's "Dawn-man" was born, and he was praised as a heroine for his discovery. This is what commonly became known as Piltdown Man.

It wasn't until nineteen fifty-three that Dawson's findings were exposed as fraud. Scientists revealed that the bone pieces were stained to make them look older, and the teeth were from an orangutan.

As the truth began to shed light on this lie, Dawson's other archeological finds were scrutinized. Forty of his other discoveries were proved to be forgeries.

For forty years he had fooled the world and the brightest minds of his day with his elegant lies. His quest was to prove that Darwin's theory was correct, and that life had originated from the United Kingdom.

Blinded by his desire for fame, he never thought his scam would be found out. But instead of becoming famous, he became infamous. His faulty reasoning hurt the lives of countless people who believed his lies. People relied on his work as evidence when it was not worth its weight in sand. Dawson's Piltdown Lie led many people to believe his lies and not see the truth.

Lies are like a bobsled. When they were first invented, they didn't have breaks and the only control riders had was only to lean left or right.

Just like you can't stop a bobsled after it starts its trip down the hill, you can't stop a lie after it is told. Once someone sets a lie in motion, it picks up speed and can only be partially steered. It becomes a destructive force that can injure others.

Like Dawson, some lies can hurt and deceive for years, destroying trust over decades and creating division and divisive acts.

A lie can destroy your credibility and create a shadow over your previous accomplishments.

It is difficult to discuss our thirty-seventh president, Richard Nixon, without mentioning the Watergate Scandal, an illegal political scandal covered up with layers of lies that led to his resignation.

The shadow of Watergate has overcast many of the good

things Nixon accomplished while in office. He ended the U.S. involvement in the Vietnam War, constructed the anti-ballistic missile treaty with the Soviet Union and China, enforced desegregation in southern schools, began the war on cancer, presided over the Apollo II moon landing, and he was reelected in the country's largest landslide election in U.S. history.

Just like Nixon's reputation, it's difficult to see the good that has been done by someone when they have scared their reputation through betrayal and lies.

Men today, who continue to advance their lives with lies, will find a trail of pain left in their wake. The people who tend to get hurt the most are usually the ones closest to them.

When men lie, they create and set in motion the very pain they wanted to protect from their loved ones. Despite this pain, men continue to lie. They continue to think of more reasons to excuse their destructive behaviors.

Having the wisdom to think forward, exploring what the potential consequences will be, can save you and those you love from a lot of pain. You can choose whatever you want to do, if it does not hurt another person directly, but to directly hurt someone is never acceptable.

Most men fall into the indirect category of causing pain to others through their choices and actions. Is this acceptable? If you don't care about the indirect impact on those close to you, then choose what you want to do.

Notice that I didn't say if you don't care about the indirect impact on those you "love." I didn't say that because that's like using a double negative. You can't choose to not care and to love at the same time. It's one or the other.

People don't like to be told no. Who has the right to tell me what to do, anyway? No one. Many may offer suggestions that can help. It's up to you to listen or not. It's not simply about my right to choose. It's also about the consequences of my choices.

For instance, there are no rules or laws that say that of-age adults cannot drink alcohol. No one is going to tell you that you can't drink, that is unless you have proven to make poor decisions and have abused this right.

If you have been recklessly driving under the influence, had accidents, or have hurt others, you have proven that you cannot make good, rational decisions regarding your drinking. You cannot control yourself! After it has been concluded you have a drinking problem, others may ask you to stop drinking for the benefit of not hurting your children, family, or anyone else.

When your choices become a competition between a loved one's best interest and your selfish gain, then yes, others will tell you no. This is not only for your sake but for theirs.

Even after facing the negative consequences of your actions, you still may choose poorly again, but it will come with a more severe consequence if you do. When the lies have become so big and have become who you are, then how can others trust you?

Men have been given responsibility, some responsibility may be small and some great. When our personal choices for pleasure compete with the greater good, we prove our irresponsibility and our immaturity.

Being responsible doesn't compete with being a man - it complements being a man. Being responsible means you're accountable for what you do.

A man who is accountable for his actions knows the value of having others behind him, his team. He knows that life's too important to do things alone. With the advice of good friends, a spouse who loves you, and others in the community that care for you, you can create a winning team.

Of course, you have a chance to win if you listen, not if you lie. Lying is like playing for the other team who is against you and your family. You may think that you're doing good when you're quickly losing.

Part of a winning team is thinking correctly and not giving in to false reasoning. Men are doing this sort of thing every day all day long thinking it's fine. If you want to win as a man and have a fighting chance to score a touchdown for your life, your family, and your career, then you must change the way you think.

When men use their brains to rationalize how to get away with wrong thinking, it is truly a waste of brainpower. You are fighting against the truth with lies. It will never work. The only way a lie can be stopped is with the truth. The only way to win is to align yourself with truth and with right thinking.

To continue thinking irrationally will only continue your negative consequences and pain.

Many men have struggled with faulty reasoning to justify why it is alright to do many of the things men often do. Here are a few of those incorrect mindsets that in the end will hurt themselves and others.

I Can Play the Field

Let's talk about one faulty way of thinking that many men in our society are dealing with. I often hear statements from men that they just want to play the field. I don't mean dating different people, that's acceptable. I'm referring to sowing their oats wildly and having sex with multiple partners.

Some of their rationalizing statements are, "How do you know what you want unless you sample it first?" "I like many flavors of ice cream." or "If I want to buy a car, shouldn't I test drive it first?"

Women are not mere food or cars, they are women. They are someone's daughter, sister, or friend. Thinking you can have multiple partners and it won't impact your current and future relationship is foolish.

Usually, the biggest excuses come from men who have been hurt. They just want to be single and fool around to escape and not deal with their past reality. Many have a fear of commitment.

Deception and lies will hurt others. They lead to taking advantage of people for your pleasure. I wish someone would step up and be a man. It's easy to go out with someone for sex, but more difficult to cultivate an actual relationship.

Don't expect the person you are with to be committed to you if you are not committed to them. If you're living in the mindset that you can "play the field" or are just waiting for someone better to come along, then so are they.

Even if you like this person, and would like to see the relationship grow more, you are hurting the chances of this happening by not being fully committed in the beginning. You set your expectations and then you lied. You wanted a shallow relationship then and now you don't? You can't have it all, you must choose.

Your expectations for the relationship can't change because

your feelings did. Some things just can't be fixed. If there is no trust in the relationship at the beginning, rebuilding that trust is an uphill battle that is hard to overcome.

I guarantee that if you start the process with meaningful conversation, things will improve. Get to know a person, how they feel about things, and their likes and dislikes. Proceed to find out their dreams and goals in life. Discover who this person "really" is.

Start to develop a relationship based on who a person is, not based on what you can get out of it. You will be amazed at the outcome of what you find.

Some people will remain casual acquaintances or friends, but then you will find that one woman that you can't live without. Invest time with her. She will be yours and you will be hers. You're building a foundation for a strong relationship where you will learn, grow, and experience love together.

Start right from the beginning and you will have a better chance to stay together. Start honestly and not with hidden agendas, not with lies. Build together from the beginning and you won't have to rebuild what another man destroys.

When you build right you are the only one with access to her heart and her full life. When you permit anyone and everyone in your life that type of full access, it's irrational to think that you can restrict that access later.

Change your mindset now and build a true relationship that will last.

I Can Control It

Men often like to be in control. It feels good to be the one behind the steering wheel or at the helm of an impressive ship.

When we are in control, it makes us feel as if everything is working out the way we want it to. We see things playing out a certain way in our minds, and we like it.

The desire to control events and to control others is tied to a person who has trust issues. If you can control the outcome, then you don't have to worry about being sad, disappointed, or betrayed.

What can we control? Are we ever in control of anything? Control is to expect a certain outcome and to do what is necessary to make sure it happens. We expect others to act in a certain way and for things to work out as we pictured.

A person who is controlling will often do whatever they have to do to make things happen the way they want. This can happen subconsciously or consciously. This type of control, to avoid being hurt or avoid negative emotions, will also limit you from experiencing the positives that come from trusting others.

There is a difference between hope and control. Unhealthy relationships control, while healthy relationships hope. Hope and faith expect things to go well but do not micro-manage the details to make sure it happens a certain way. Faith and hope expect good things, but let the details work out themselves.

Controlling partners in relationships must make sure

outcomes match what they expect. But what can be controlled in life?

Controlling other people and their actions is not a relationship. It's manipulation. Is wanting people to be robotic so you can feel safe with the result, the answer? No, it's not! It's immaturity, a faulty way of thinking, and treating other people as if they are children.

With parents, there is an amount of control we lovingly enforce until our little ones prove they can be mature enough to make their own healthy decisions. At some point, we must release the control and allow our children to properly self-guide their own lives.

Bringing this thought process and approach into an adult relationship is belittling. We can't control people, what they will say, what they will do, how they will react, or what they decide. Love demands a free choice, even if that choice is the wrong one. Forcing someone to love you is not love. Demanding someone to do something is not love, but slavery, and changes the results.

Just like we can't control people; we can't control events. No one knows what tomorrow holds. Who can control their child getting sick, losing a loved one, being a victim of a crime, or experiencing a natural disaster? No one can. We can only manage the situation the best we can. The only thing in life we can ultimately control is ourselves.

Self-control is the only controlling power you possess. It's the ability to determine your "own" thoughts and actions. How you exercise self-control or not will impact your life.

This is not the same as an addict trying to control usage. Self-control is not trying to control a substance. Self-control consists of controlling yourself, not others, or other things.

Using self-control would be resisting the urge to use a substance, and controlling your thoughts and actions that help keep you from potentially using drugs.

You can never win a match trying to control a substance. It is not an equal matchup. It's human against substance. It's uncontrollable. Giving up control and exercising self-control is the only alternative to death, pain, or bondage in addiction.

Handling a substance and thinking you can control a certain amount is faulty reasoning and you're just lying to yourself. The only thing you can control is you, to resist or give in.

Managing the outcome of using drugs through recovery and treatment is done by changing your actions, behaviors, beliefs, thoughts, and temptations.

In relationships, giving up control and exercising self-control is the catalyst for giving and receiving more love, joy, respect, and satisfaction.

To manage, unlike control, is to handle things with the skill to the best of your ability. With this comes the responsibility to treat others with care and concern in a way that reflects who you are.

When your child becomes sick, something you cannot control, you are the one that helps to handle the situation. With responsible care, you do what's best to see your child get well again. You take care of how you feel too, allowing yourself to be honest with how you feel so you can eventually help others in your family to do the same. You have managed this well.

You have a responsibility to care for your family emotionally, socially, spiritually, mentally, and physically. To deny care in any of these areas is to keep them down and hold them back.

Set an example they would want to follow and emulate.

Forcing your view or opinion on them will not work. Instead, guide them to make the best choices. Your views and opinions are ultimately expressed best by how they are lived out.

Your family needs to hear your values, but they need to see you live them out more. You can't tell your children that you want them to tell the truth as if that's what you value if you are caught constantly lying. They will know subconsciously that you value lies.

For example, you can't say that they should not use drugs or alcohol when they watch you use them all the time. They will be impacted by your negative consequences and know you lied.

Your example is priceless. It will speak to your family's future, modeling what and who you are.

Self-control, not control, will help guide you to be your best. It will keep you from the faulty thinking that you can manipulate others to do what you want them to do. Remember, the only thing you can control is you.

I Can Get Away with It

A man who thinks he can get away with something is a man already doomed to fail. This is a man who has already decided to deceive and lie.

Men often falsely think they can get away with something, though they may hardly say it directly. Indirectly, men think that they can get away with whatever they are going to do, even if they know it is wrong. If you didn't think you could get away with it, then why would you even try?

Pride swells their thinking until they feel a sense of invincibility. This feeling causes them to believe they are smarter, to some degree, than all the others that came before them. But the opposite is true.

Criminals often depict this feeling of invincibility perfectly. They think they are smarter than they are when their false pride blinds them. They make foolish mistakes that eventually lead to their demise. Just think of how many television shows are produced about criminals who have this type of thinking. It's entertaining for a reason! But many men think this way.

You may think you're different and smarter than the average Joe, and you're way too intelligent to get caught. Do you think that you can cheat on your spouse, and she will never know it? Wrong! She will know. She will intuitively pick up on how you are carrying yourself and how you are treating her. She wonders why you're not in the mood as often as you usually are, and she has a bad feeling about something. You can't escape it.

Don't believe the lie that doing wrong will be worth it. Even if you are crafty enough to keep some of these so-called hidden activities from her, she will know. Her intuition will pick up on it.

The reason you can't get away with anything is that you're an influencer. You may not even know this, but whether you like it or not, you are one.

Influencers are meant to be seen; they cannot hide things. Others who depend on them watch their every move, including spouses, children, sisters, brothers, and friends.

With today's technology, getting away with something

wrong is extremely difficult than it used to be. Before everyone had a recording device in their hand, it may have been easier. Nowadays, everyone is like a film director looking for their next big hit.

The worst part about your deceptive actions is that you know it's wrong. You know you're a fraud, a liar. You are giving off signals to everyone around you that you're a player. They may not say anything to you, but they know it. You are poorly influencing others' opinions by being a bad example. The example you are setting is hideous.

You're trying to convince others that your behavior is tolerable and acceptable when it's not. You're trying to influence others that living a lie is beneficial when it's not.

Maybe you're thinking of moving on from a marriage because you're interested in someone else. Someone once told me that the grass always looks greener on the other side of the fence, but it still needs mowing. It may seem better temporarily. It may look better temporarily. But, when you start putting in the work on something new, or someone new, you will find everyone requires something more to make it work.

It's not worth it! You won't ever fully get away with it. You will just trade your current problems with a set of new ones. Nothing will change because you are still the same liar you were before.

You are the same person and will bring the same issues with you into the new situation. Thinking you can get away with it is a cop-out. It's a way to fail before you even start. This mindset will only bring defeat, not victory. It will bring sorrow, not happiness or joy.

The only redeeming effect is when you get caught and face

the consequences. Then, at least those watching you can see the truth that it does not pay to lie, cheat, and steal. Your pain might be their gain.

Don't continue with lies but commit to being honest, open, and genuine. Don't try to get away with anything. Be a real man who faces things honestly with nothing to hide.

My Life is My Own

Think about it: everyone has come from somewhere. Even if your birth parents are unknown to you, or they were unfavorable in your sight, you still came from people, humans.

You may have heard it said, owe no man anything but love. That is the greatest responsibility we have as human beings, to owe others love. Not necessarily trust, companionship, or even friendship, but love.

Someone probably took some time to plan out your existence - your birth. You may have been born out of adversity and see the hardship you had to face as something good, or even something evil, but you exist. Think about how many babies were chosen not to enter the world. Someone didn't make that choice about you.

The very fact that you exist is proof that you should have some gratitude to be alive, maybe not towards your genetic parents, but to people in general.

Gratitude comes from a Latin word meaning pleasing. You should have an attitude of pleasing based on a grateful perspective that comes with a responsibility to pay others back in a positive way.

Thinking your life is only your own is like thinking that you are alone in the universe. You are not alone! There are at least seven billion other people on earth in your universe.

If your life is not your own, then whose is it? Your life is yours to manage, yes. You are responsible for your thoughts, actions, and how you affect others in the world. This responsibility to others is seen daily in our families, written in our laws, and lived throughout the world.

Be a fool and watch what happens. Foolish acts that hurt others will have serious consequences in our society. We all have a social responsibility to not harm the wellbeing of others and treat our family with an expected standard.

Don't believe me? Ask any addict who was using drugs at home while they were supposed to be responsibly watching and protecting their children. Child Protective Services most likely came and took their children out of their homes. Why? We all are responsible for others, but parents are especially responsible to protect their children.

There is an expectation in how we are to treat others - a standard. Don't know what that standard is? Cross the line and you will quickly learn what it is.

A fiduciary is a person that has a legal obligation to exercise a certain amount of care and responsibility entrusted to them for another. You are always a fiduciary, to yourself first and then to others. You have one life to live. Don't believe the lie that it's your life all alone to live the way you want.

You have choices and a say in your life, but it is much bigger than that. Your choices and decisions impact, so choose well.

Make choices not just for yourself, but for your family, friends, faith, and others.

Choose to live your life in a way that is beneficial to everyone, including yourself. Live your life as a steward of it, a manager not an owner. In all you do, remember the responsibility of care and the debt of gratitude you owe.

Your life is a lease, so make the best use of your lease, because no one knows when their lease is set to expire.

I Don't Have to Grow Up

Another defective way of thinking is that you don't have to grow up. This is just an excuse to act immature and do whatever you want. Don't give in to this kind of thinking, you will fill your life with regret.

A life full of regret is a life lived backward, like someone stuck in reverse. We were never meant to live life backward, but to live forward. It's like accidentally putting your car in reverse when you fully expected it to be in drive. You will end up where you never wanted to go.

I remember a toy commercial growing up that said, "I don't want to grow up. I'm a Toys "R" Us kid." It seems harmless, but an adult who doesn't want to grow up never fully develops their character. Someone who is not growing is guaranteed to have regrets. It's not normal to stay put and not grow.

Life speaks this lesson everywhere, all the time. Everything living grows. Small saplings grow to great trees, tiny tadpoles to frogs, caterpillars to butterflies, and seeds to flowers, fruits, and vegetables.

A human is no different in that you will grow, whether you want to or not. Your body will grow and hopefully, you will mature simultaneously with age. It is alright on occasion to act younger and enjoy yourself, but someone who acts like that all the time is stuck.

Just like a seed, which needs water and a good location to grow, a man needs truth, character, and a good environment to express that truth so that he can grow properly.

Physically, we all grow and that is easy to see. It's unnatural to not grow physically, but not growing in character, as a man, has become common.

You may be small in stature, and tall in character. You may be physically tall, but small as a real man.

Growing mentally, morally, spiritually, and relationally is where our character is developed. You may have heard it said that it takes a man to raise a man. If this is true, then why do we have so many men that are acting like children? How can we raise men if we are not men ourselves?

Men are often content growing physically and even mentally while neglecting their moral, spiritual, and relational growth. They become stunted and stuck, and are grown men outwardly, but little children in their relationships, decision making, and how they approach their life.

A real man is a man not just outwardly but inwardly and all around. The last thing that makes a man a man is his physical appearance.

The wrapping may look nice, but what's good may only be on the surface, and a host of other problems may be covered up. It's like an undercooked meat pie that looks done. One bite and you spit it out because it is disgusting and raw! A superficial failure. It needs to be fully cooked and so do we as men.

You look like a man, smell like a man, and feel like a man, now act like it! Be the moral and spiritual figure our society needs you to be. Only when we are fully developed can we offer something useful to society and others. We must move beyond being the outward wrappings of a liar to something much deeper, becoming a balanced man of truth.

Be the father your children need you to be, not the one who makes them desire to be orphans. Be the husband your wife needs you to be, not the person who consistently lets her down, cheats on her behind her back, and continues to cause pain.

The wrapper may not be ideal, but it's what's inside that counts more. If you have grown deeply morally, spiritually, and relationally then you offer so much more to others and society than the average man.

You offer trust that brings security. Love that never fails. A peace that calms the most difficult of life's storms. A provision that can be counted on. Hope that helps to develop our dreams. The encouragement that gives us strength. The wisdom that protects our life. A joy that unites others and binds us together. A faith that inspires us to be better. A truth that we can build our lives on.

So yes, you do need to grow up. Our life depends on it. So, does yours.

I Can Hide It

Nothing is worse than the hidden agenda of a liar. He thinks he can hide this and may even do a good job at masking it, but eventually, his intentions will become known.

When someone has a hidden motive and a plan to accomplish something that's shadowed in lies, it becomes a dagger of pain for those it is aimed at.

This pain starts with finding out that someone who you thought was honorable, was dishonorable. You thought they were for you but found out they were for themselves, and you were just in their way.

The longer lies and hidden agendas stay hidden, the more pain it inflicts. It's like cancer when treated early, can often be removed, but if symptoms are ignored or it's found too late, it can cause more pain and suffering. Now, it will take a miracle to heal.

A hidden agenda is not a nice surprise. The liar with an ulterior motive is thinking of only himself. His gift, a twisted surprise, is only pain and you're caught off guard by his real intent.

You may find it hard to believe this was his agenda all along. He is somewhere in between a relationship terrorist and a felonious friend. He may have intended to destroy your life as part of his original agenda, or you just happened to be in his way.

Your pain was just a byproduct of his plan. The ultimate lie is the hidden agenda left unexposed, a lie of mammoth proportions.

It's only a matter of time before this hidden motive is exposed. The sooner the better. The longer it takes to reveal the truth the worse it gets. It feeds on time and grows accordingly. The larger it gets, the bigger the lies become, and the larger the degree of pain it will inflict.

Men with hidden agendas are either extremely selfish or plain evil. Thinking you can hide this corrupt way forever is a fallacy and will eventually be revealed. When it comes out, the pain will come like a shark attack on an unbeknownst swimmer. It will be a total shock to your system.

If you have been the recipient of a man's hidden plan, then you know exactly what this feels like. The pain of such betrayal and lies breaks trust and pulls people apart. You're left in the aftermath of this disaster and all you can do is pick up the pieces and start over.

If he comes clean, exposes the false thinking, and reveals his true intent, then the surprise is gone, and you know his true intentions. Even if he doesn't change, at least you won't be strung along on his kamikaze mission. You'll be free from his lies and his sinister warped thinking.

I Can Keep a Secret

What is a secret? It's when you keep some form of knowledge or truth from others. Secrets are also keeping something from someone's view, hiding something from their sight.

What is it that you don't want them to know or find out? Is it something about you, or something you have done? What are you hiding that you don't want others to know? Why is it a secret?

Secrets are hidden lies with underlying motives. Societies, with the word secret in them, are there to hide their agendas. If they were truly exposed, the truth would probably leave us speechless.

Watch out for these types of secrets on a massive level institutionally. They dive deeper into bigger lies, wider deception, and hiding lots of truth from society. They must be very secretive to protect their lies.

Some organizations may look like they are doing some good deeds, but secretly they are protecting and covering up dangerous activity. Their good deeds are blinding people from seeing their actual crimes.

Openness and accountability develop trust and safety. Secrets and lies develop doubt and a sense of danger.

The word secret originates from the Latin word meaning to set apart, divide, or to exclude. In a secret, we hope to exclude others from knowing the truth. We divide the truth into parts and only show others what we want them to see. This takes that which is hidden from the knowledge and view of others. By separating the truth from those we don't want to know it, we create a secret, a lie.

But are all secrets lies? Not necessarily. It depends on what you are protecting. Are you protecting yourself and your actions, or are you protecting others from harm? Are you protecting people, or are you protecting your guilty conduct?

Keeping a secret about where in your home you keep your

valuables is a safe way to protect assets, but keeping the secret of where you stashed money you robbed from others is not.

Keeping a secret from your children that protects them from the harsh realities of life is a way to preserve their innocence, but keeping a secret from your children just to protect yourself from your bad actions is not.

Secrets often weave lies into them. These lies help keep hidden what we don't want others to know. When someone is keeping a secret from you, it tends to subconsciously bother you. You can feel it! You know something is wrong. It's annoying and even uncomfortable to be kept in the dark about something.

As humans, we connect with people through trust and being open with them, and it hurts to be disconnected by secrets. We were meant to know the truth, not to be kept from it.

Sometimes the truth we are meant to know needs to be revealed to us gradually. We may not be able to handle the full exposure of truth all at once, and that's ok. When we have become used to secrets and lies, the full truth can feel like touching a hot oven. It will leave us with a truth burn. Ouch!

Sometimes the truth is covered up and needs to be exposed and uncovered. Truth revealed gradually is not keeping a secret, it is simply an unveiling of the truth. This helps to make sure we are ready and can handle more truth. Sometimes people can't know the entire truth. They may not be able to handle it or may mishandle it if they had it.

Wherever there is a secret, there is a reason for keeping it. Secrets always equal hidden motives, which can be acceptable or unacceptable.

Secrets to protect your behavior are usually for the wrong reasons. Keeping a secret about plans to rob a bank, to hide illegal activity and wrong thinking, is unacceptable. Keeping a secret about an affair to hide your broken promises is also unacceptable.

Acceptable motivations for keeping secrets are those kept protecting innocent lives, sometimes even yourself. This is usually the only rationale that is worthy of keeping a secret. Protecting loved ones often means, at times, we must keep a secret. It's a secret out of love that is focused on helping others stay safe.

A liar can't protect anyone but himself. His lies have tainted his point of view, and he may even be deceived that he is helping you, while only helping himself.

Personal secrets are often unlocked through trust. When I first started dating my wife, I had many secrets. If I were to tell her all of them at once, she would have been overwhelmed. She had some secrets, too.

It's good practice to build trust with someone before you trust them with your secrets. That's not keeping a secret, but rather protecting yourself from others who have not earned that access.

Today, people easily give away the combination of their heart and mind's treasury, later to realize that the person they trusted with their deepest secrets betrayed them.

As my wife and I grew in our relationship, we slowly began to be open about who we were, what we believed, and our dreams. We committed ourselves to each other as a foundation to build trust.

Sex before commitment always equals handing over full access to who you are. It's like giving someone your bank account numbers and social security number. If you can't trust them with those, why would you trust them with your heart?

Watch out for the man who secretly only wants full access to your heart for his hidden agenda, to fulfill his sexual desire. You mean nothing to him! You were just part of the hidden agenda in his secret. The truth he is hiding is that he is a thief and a liar.

A man who has access to everything about you immediately does not care about you. He is selfish. If he cared about you, he would embrace the true mystery of who you are. With time, he can carefully find out more about you, enjoying the beautiful adventure. Gradually being open more and more, you will establish trust.

A mystery is something hard to explain or understand. It must be researched with time to gain a better understanding. It's not a secret with hidden motives but takes skill, understanding, and time to fully understand.

Be a mystery, not a secret. Be someone who others want to find the truth about, not someone full of lies. Unacceptable secrets and lies produce deception. Deception takes on an element of truth, making you believe it is true when it is wrapped around lies and secrets.

Do you believe he loves you when he does not? He brings you flowers and always buys dinner, but is it to mask his hidden agenda to use you for his selfish needs?

Do you believe that the secret society you are part of is doing lots of good for children, and therefore, must have good intentions? You may not be privy to what is going on, that there are deep dark actions taking place against innocent people and covering up their crimes.

Deception can be twisted with good deeds, which can make it very confusing to see the reality of what is true.

When I was young, a wicked person was putting razor blades

in Halloween candy. My parents had to go through all our candy and inspect it for razor blades. Deception is just like what this horrible person did. What you see on the outside is sweet, wrapped up nicely, but in the end, it hurts, steals, and kills.

In our society, men are hiding from the truth, keeping secrets, and playing games with people's lives to hide their ugly actions done in secret. Don't fall for it.

Live in the light of day, not the darkness of secrets. Light exposes darkness, that's why light and truth are equal. Truth seeks to be open, exposed by the light and does not hide in the shadows. Truth has no secret agenda for personal gain or pleasure.

"Truth" may be a mystery to be discovered, but it is not a secret. It's open, honest, and straightforward for all to embrace and see. We need men who seek the truth, not secrets; embrace openness, not secrecy; and are dedicated to being a part of our lives and our families in truth.

If men continue to embrace faulty reasons to lie and keep secrets, they will never discover their true self and its benefits on those they love. Instead, in their lies, they will continue to believe false reasonings for what they are doing and continue to spread the pain they cause.

The pain we are causing must stop. We need to become something more, someone new.

Questions for Self-Reflection

What are some things you have believed in that you later realized were not true?

How have you been mistreated?

How have you not grown up?

Have you ever lived as if your life was all your own? How?

What secrets have you kept that need to be exposed?

9

A New Man

So ultimately, why do men lie? We have looked at many reasons why men lie, but it all comes down to the fact that they have believed a lie, and in many cases, have become a lie.

Men are deceived. They have believed that the advantage of having money, sex, position, power, or fame, is worth their lies. Rather than embracing the truth about who they "really" are, they would rather believe the outcome of their lies.

Some lies men have believed include:

- Having money will change everything for the better.
- The more women I can be with physically will give me an expert point of view on the type of woman I want for life.
- If I can just get that promotion at work, I will have become a success.
- All I need is to be in control, and if I can control everything, nothing will take me by surprise.

- If everyone likes me and thinks highly of me, it will make me feel better about myself.
- If failing at everything is always my outcome, then why even try?

Lies. These are all lies that men often believe and live. Within the consequences of these lies, men receive the message that they are failures.

I read an interesting fact once that 40 percent of people lie on their resume. It seems the statistics get worse when looking for a relationship, than when looking for a job. It's estimated that 90 percent of people looking for an online romance lie about themselves to look better. Every 10 minutes, 60 percent of the population feel the need to lie about something.

Those who lie, lie so much they can no longer tell when someone is telling a lie. To them, the truth sounds wrong. They have become accustomed to the counterfeit lies for so long that it feels real to them, and the truth feels unreal.

How do you know if someone is lying? It starts with you being an honest person first. You will not recognize a lie if you're a liar. Only the truth can expose a lie.

It can often be hard to be a human lie detector. Either you're a liar and can't recognize lies, or you're so honest you expect others to be the same way. It may be difficult for a person who is honest to believe they are being lied to even when it feels wrong. Your loyalty may get in the way of recognizing a lie.

People expect others to treat them the way they treat others. We often deal with people the way we want to be dealt with. That's why betrayal hurts so much! We don't want to believe it. We don't want to admit it or face the realization of what it means to us.

It can be devastating when you discover that a person who was supposed to have your best interest in mind, only had their own selfish needs as their motive. You may find out that a friend was an enemy, or a family member was a foe.

But, when we finally realize that the person, we thought was for us lied, and was against us, then we can begin to see what's true.

The only thing worse than lying is to be on the other end of someone's lie. It hurts to be the one who is receiving the pain from the actions of another when you did nothing wrong yourself. That's why truth is the only remedy for a lie.

Only truth can help begin healing from a lie. Truth is the salve that heals wounds inflicted from lies. Give it time to work. It's not immediate but will be a process. The truth from the offender, or the truth from another, will help start the healing process.

Forgiving does not mean trusting, but it is essential if you want to heal. You must release the toxins injected through lies or they will keep hurting you.

Without forgiving the one who lied, you continue to let their lies hurt you. Let someone else vindicate you. You need to heal.

If you don't heal, the very lie that poisoned you will draw in more poison and more lies. The very thing you want to get away from, you will invite in. It will constantly keep you trapped in a fog, looking for a way out. Unforgiveness may pull you down so far that you become what you can't forgive - a liar.

Forgiving will allow you to let it go. It's a choice to not get even or to vindicate yourself. You will leave that to someone else, while you claim your freedom, you're healing.

This is not freedom from the person who hurt you, but from the pain and the damage done by their lies. In some cases, separation from the liar may be needed.

Change is what is needed most. In the absence of change, you run the risk of repeating the past. We are who we are, and if we are to be different, then we need to change and change sincerely.

Men need to transform and be different. This starts with changing the way we think. Lying is not much different than being an addict. Lying is a drug to the mind like other drugs are to the body. When someone continues to use drugs, despite the negative consequences, they are an addict or on their way to becoming one.

A lying addict is someone who lies, despite the negative outcome. An addict likes the temporary feeling of their drug, even if the reality afterward has a negative impact.

They keep doing it for two reasons. One reason is the addictive nature and pleasure they receive from the drug. The other reason is the negative consequence in their thinking does not outweigh the temporary pleasure they feel.

At some point, the addict and the liar become one. They believe there is no negative consequence to their use, or that it's too minimal to worry about. They have believed and become a lie.

The first step to recovery for the addict and the liar is always the same - acknowledge the truth. Not your version of the truth, the "real" truth.

Once this truth is embraced, freedom begins. The truth really will set you free! It will make you a new man. A new man is a man who gives up control but maintains self-control. He is fully accepting of the responsibility of his thoughts and actions. He understands how his life choices affect others and chooses to live to better their lives. A new man is a man who is in total control of himself, yet he is also completely surrendered to God. He is aware that he cannot control anything beyond himself. Only in his surrender to God are things, that are out of his control, given over to a true higher power. Truth will always lead you on a path to victorious living.

So how can a man stuck in lies become a new man? It starts with acknowledgement.

Acknowledgment

The first step to freedom and truth is to acknowledge the error, the lie. Decide to talk to someone who values truth. Tell them how you have lied, or how you have believed a lie, and don't hold back anything. Everything you hold back from confessing will come back later to haunt you.

Some people may need more time to fully confess, as they have been living with their lies for months, even years. They may need time to peel back the layers. It's alright to peel the lie off like an onion, but I prefer the Band-Aid method to get it over with quickly.

When someone has lied for a long time, they can forget a lot of the lies they have told. As they begin to open themselves up, they may remember more and more of their lies as the process continues. Be patient and go slow if you need to.

The key here is to go from denial to acknowledging the truth. This may seem easy, but the hardest step for many to take is acknowledging their error.

Denial is not easily overcome, men love their comfort zones, but this is where you begin to see the light of truth. To admit you were wrong about something takes humility. Pride will keep many men from admitting they were wrong, even long after they realized they had an issue.

It's important to talk out loud about it! You need to hear it with your ears, and it needs to come out of your mouth. This may sound weird, but it is true. You won't begin to believe something to be true until you hear it in your words, with your tongue, and in your language.

Your lies started in thought, moved through your lips, and then to action. A lie that started in thought was reinforced by speaking it and then acted on. This is the same way truth needs to be reinforced, by speaking it and acting upon it.

This is like backing a car out of the garage. You can't have it in drive mode, you must put it in reverse. The action of reversing your lies starts by agreeing to talk to someone. Then with your mouth, you discuss it in your words, while backing up carefully.

When you start opening-up about all your lying while embracing your new honesty, you begin to think about things differently.

Just like backing up your car, you're looking back at what you did in your rear-view mirror. You're discussing how your lies impacted others around you with your side mirrors. When you're done and ready to move to the next step, put your life back in drive and move forward.

You're about to move from lying to being honest. It won't be as easy as just shifting your car in gear. Your resolve will be tested. You will want to stay in the past and not move forward. The change may feel uncomfortable and the view temporarily limiting, but it is about to get so much better for you.

Commitment

A word many men like to avoid is commitment. This is the key to the ignition of your new car - a new man, a new you. You decided to trade in that old clunker. While in denial, you believed that it was the best and most comfortable car there was, just like you thought you were the best version of yourself. You were delusional.

You are now ready for a new car, a new "you." It's going to take commitment to make this change stick. This commitment will ignite the passion and willpower necessary within you, reminding you daily of your new choices. This dedication will pay off as you turn a new leaf and embrace your honest self.

Commitment is the glue that bonds your thoughts and decisions to your new actions. You will begin to see things differently. It won't take long to begin reaping the benefits of honesty.

Your relationships will begin to take on more meaning. A new reputation will begin to be built. People will begin to see you differently, but you still have a lot to prove to rebuild trust with others. Be patient. You're setting a new foundation.

Some people, depending on their perspectives and the impact of your lies on their life, may need more time to trust you. That's why it's so important to continue to stay committed and do whatever is necessary to help reinforce your change.

This commitment is like joining the Army. You have signed the agreement to enlist, but you have no clue what you're getting yourself into. It's all good just hang in there.

I remember the night that I joined the Army as clear as day. I boarded a plane to Texas, a place I had never been to where I knew no one. I felt lost and alone but meeting a few other guys on the plane who also were joining the Army gave me some comfort.

Getting off a plane, I found myself in the biggest airport I had ever seen. Not knowing where to go, the group that I had met on the plane followed each other until we found a man waiting for us in a military uniform, who escorted us onto a bus.

It was the middle of the night and so dark. We couldn't remember the way to the Army base even if we tried. At least we got to know each other on the bus and felt more comfortable with some familiarity. The problem was that when we got there, they pulled each of us out separately and shaved our heads. We couldn't recognize anyone anymore. Again, we felt confused, lost, and alone.

A man committing, from being a liar to embracing the truth, may feel similar. A little confused, lost, and all alone. Everything he knows is now being turned upside down.

It can be overwhelming and exciting at the same time. Your

life is getting set up correctly, you're just not used to it yet. Good things are going to happen, but it won't come without a cost.

Now is not the time to go AWOL because it is going to be somewhat painful and uncomfortable. It will be challenging and there will be times when you want to quit. Press on.

Each day that passes by, you're becoming more skilled and in better shape. You're developing friendships with those who have the same goal as you.

Your mental focus is getting sharper, and you are getting stronger. You're realizing that you cannot do this all alone. You need a team to win.

Accountability

A single rope can be strong or weak, depending on its quality and integrity. Take that same rope and wrap it around a few more pieces of rope and you have just caused a major reinforcement of strength - that's accountability.

Accountability allows others to wrap their opinion and counsel around you. It lets others ask how you are doing and check in on you whenever they want to. This will always help you to stay vigilant, on guard, and protect your new identity. It's a powerful reinforcement to your new commitment.

Building a good reputation is like finding new treasure, but it also must be protected from thieves and liars. Pirates will stop at nothing to get their hands on your value.

How important is this change to you? Is your commitment weak or strong? If it is strong, you will do whatever is necessary to protect your new-found treasure. Add personal bodyguards if you must, but you're not going to allow just anyone to have free access.

Accountability will help you to be strong during adversity. When life gets hard, and it will, we need others to help us from giving up. Find people who are looking in the same direction as you, who can help you stay on course.

The Army was not easy and wanting to give up goes through everyone's mind often at the beginning of the hard training. Ralph, a fellow private in the military, was assigned to the same barracks as me. He was in the bunk above mine, and we got to know each other well. We often encouraged each other to continue the course, and most importantly, to not give up.

With no one to talk to, who knows if I would have been able to keep my commitment. It was much easier to face all the challenges we had to endure knowing I was not alone.

You cannot do this all by yourself. There will be circumstances that will come your way to challenge your resolve. If you go about this all alone, you may not make it. It's always better to go into battle with other brothers-in-arms, a committed group of like-minded individuals who have your back and won't leave a man behind.

With this accountability in place, you will have the ability to face whatever comes against your new commitment. The challenge now is to continue doing the right thing and be the new you.

Don't let pride separate you from the pack. It's easy to think you know what's best when you're starting to see some progress.

This can be easily demonstrated in the mental health field when a diagnosis is given to someone, and medicine is prescribed for treating a chemical imbalance. The person realizes their situation is not improving and agrees to the treatment and medication.

After a few weeks, they begin to see improvement and begin thinking they no longer need the medication. Despite others who advise against it, many people stop taking their medications. Their brain tricks them into thinking they don't need it. To keep their progress, they must trust those around them and their doctor to continue treatment.

Just like them, your new identity can't ignore those you're accountable to. Pride will try to bring you back to total self-reliance. If you let it, you will find yourself back where you began.

Accountability is your medication for character imbalance. Taken regularly, it will reinforce your new changed self.

Persistence

Keep on, keeping on. You made your decision to be an honest man and dedicated yourself to change. You have allowed others to help you in your new quest for truth. What's next? Stay the course.

Be persistent! This is where you nail down your progress broadly and your resolve is strengthened. You have passed many challenges that have tried to pull you back to the person you were and have proven yourself to be a worthy opponent of lies.

You are seeing the benefits of truth in your life and like it. You are looking for new ways to lessen the burden of fighting off lies and to make things a little easier.

Benefits of your persistence begin to pay off, and you kick into the next gear and continue to advance. Wisdom develops and you've decided that you can no longer associate with known liars. You distance yourself from those holding you back from being your best and all those trying to pull you back into your old ways.

It's time to lighten the load you're carrying. It's time to hang around those people who value truth and honesty, not those who steal it from others.

People want to be around others like them. Being around someone who constantly sees things differently than you do will weigh you down and drain you emotionally.

I'm not advocating for racial divide, the opposite. To open yourself up to people of differing backgrounds, cultures, and interests who believe as you do have significant value. Those who have their unique perspective will add value to what you have.

Old friends that liked the old you, the liar, will want the old you back and not the new you. The honest man will expose their lies and create a sense of vulnerability in them, making them uncomfortable.

They will want you to be more like them again, which makes them feel comfortable. In every thought, comment, and action, they will continuously work against you until you give in. They don't have a choice, it's who they are.

Remember, we discussed that you cannot control them, but

you can exercise self-control and distance yourself. If you don't, they will be your eventual downfall.

Even a tough rope, strengthened by accountability, will eventually break if constantly exposed to drops of acid. That's what they are to your new truth. In everything they do, they constantly drip acid on what you have accomplished. Sometimes they fully know what they are doing, but most often they are just being themselves - liars.

Their persistence will pay off for them if you are not persistent in your new truth. Persistence is about strengthening your change, despite adversity, and not weakening it. This is where you will make significant changes and growth.

Through wisdom, you set the necessary boundaries to protect what you value. No one leaves their doors unlocked when they know thieves are in the area. So why would you?

It's never wrong to protect yourself from negative influences. Only from a place of protected persistence and wisdom can you later offer help to those who want to change. But right now, hold your course.

You need to safeguard your truth and the new you. There is a lot more truth to learn and you have a long way to "grow." You have just opened the door to truth and shut the door to your old lies.

Your commitment has been reinforced with accountability and you have started to build on your new foundation with wise decisions. As you begin to grow confidently in the freedom of being a real man of truth, you will want more of it. That's exactly what should happen.

You have found something good, and you want more of it.

Hunger For Truth

Hungering for truth, adding more value to your treasure, is the stage that completely changes your life. You have found how precious honesty can be, and realized there are more riches of truth out there and are hungry for it.

You have starved the old bad habits, ways, addiction, and lies, and they are barely alive and almost dead. You feed on as much truth as you can get. You begin to grow and to change like you never thought you could. You're on a "truth" journey. There is no holding you back now.

It's all about how hungry you are for the truth. Maybe you're comfortable with just being an honest man and not lying anymore. You may be happy with that, but there is so much more out there.

It will require you to dig deeper, but you will find hidden gems of truth out there. Are you hungry enough to go for it?

To add to your treasure vault will not only benefit your life but everyone you influence for good. Your appetite has changed. You used to feed yourself with the fast food of lies, and now, you're getting used to a healthy meal of truth.

You used to crave junk food that had very little nutritional value, but now, you're craving healthier and more beneficial food. You have more energy and endurance, and you're no longer weighed down by the lies of your past.

People have recognized your changes and appreciate what

you have done. You love the new you and how it makes you feel. You're never going back to that life of lies again.

You have seen too many benefits from truth to return and go back. The rewards have been more than you could have hoped for.

You're closer to friends and family. Your wife loves the new you and shows her appreciation often. Your children are your biggest fans as they grow and want to learn all they can about truth to be just like you.

You just can't keep this to yourself anymore. You want others to know of your success, and you want to help them move from lying to the truth too. You now want others to experience the same rewards you have. You want to help them be free from all the lies that are holding them back.

You're open and honest and are experiencing an entirely new life that's now filled with satisfaction and joy for you, and all those you influence.

Reproducing

The final stage of evolution of the new man is "adaptation", then "reproduction."

Adaptation is where others begin to admire the new you and want to be like you. They begin to adopt traits that you emulate.

Like the child who imitates their father or the teenager who is trying to be just like their sports hero, trying out their every move, your name and your reputation precede you.

People identify your name with who you are now, not what you used to do. Hearing your name brings a sense of warmth and calmness to people. They want what you have.

You're not stingy. They can have it too. You are helping them to be accountable in their new decisions. Adaptation has taken place.

They will take on their unique challenges, make their commitments themselves, be accountable, and persist and grow. Having that same thirst and hunger for truth that you do; they will follow your example and path to be an honest and real man.

This is where reproduction has taken place. As they begin to help others and reproduce this cycle, then you have been replicated. A legacy is born.

There is no greater legacy than a father passing down his wholesome character to the next generation through his children. Giving the best of who you are, and seeing it alive in your children, will allow your treasure to carry on.

If you remain a liar and act accordingly, they will do whatever they can to forget about your existence.

Your reputation, as a man of truth, is part of your current reward, and your legacy is what you will leave behind for others to follow and remember you by.

There is nothing better in life than to have lived well and for others to follow in your footsteps. Be a real and honest man who others can become like and reap all the benefits that come with it.

The worst thing a man can do is to replicate himself while he is still a liar. He will just increase dysfunction and leave behind more pain. We don't need clones but transformed people who think for themselves.

It's time for men everywhere to embrace truth and abandon their lies. It's not easy, but it is always worth the pain you must face being a better man.

In the end, the pain you will endure to change will never be more than the many rewards you and others will gain.

Turning Pain To Gain

We all love a great comeback story when a "nobody" becomes a "somebody." We love it when against all odds, someone breaks through our expectations to be much more than we ever imagined.

These stories make some of the greatest movies. Why? Because there is something in all of us that admires the heroism, endurance, and turnaround of a man or woman we didn't know had it in them. It inspires hope in us.

With this hope, then maybe we too can turn around and be different. A true "Rocky" moment, where in the middle of losing, we find the internal strength to be a winner.

Many of us have heard the debate of nature versus nurture. Nature blames our environment and circumstances that are out of our control and that surrounds us while growing up. Nurture deals with how we were treated growing up and its positive or negative impact on our lives.

There is both truth and lies packed into these theories. Nurture by itself will not guarantee that you will become a better person. You can have all the loving attention in the world and still grow up feeling inadequate or that you're missing something.

Other people treating you well may help to set a good example for you but will never take the place of your journey of personal growth. There is no guarantee from good nurturing that you will turn out to be, or to do, good yourself. Others cannot keep you from your struggles and adversity. Most people feel that better nurturing does offer the chances for better successful outcomes, and I agree.

Nurturing parents often overstep and enable you so that you never develop the fight that is necessary for reaching your destiny. I agree that it's less painful than dealing with the harsh environment of nature, but over nurturing can also create a sense of numbness within. Laziness can keep you from trying.

How about nature? Our environment is not under our control. Does it shape us and make us who we are? In part, it will have an impact on us, but it is more how we respond to it that determines our path in life, than the mere environment itself.

Many people develop a defensive nature from constantly resisting their negative environment. Or they just give in and accept who they are told to be. They let the forces and pain around them define them, living life as a lie.

It may be hard, or outright impossible, but it's within that painful environment where you can begin to thrive. Not accepting the status quo, but resisting it develops strength through that resistance.

This fight makes you a fighter with the strength of a winner, who is defeating every negative element of his or her environment.

Some men, instead of developing an internal strength to

resist, develop a hardness instead. This outer shell protects them from their environmental factors. The problem is that this shell will also keep them from growing and experiencing anything good and new.

The place of denial is a place of hardness, protecting you from all that's bad and equally, from all that's good. You can see this hardness in people who are mean, ugly, and bitter at everyone and anyone. They are allowing the bad things of their environment to continue to hurt them, as well as also missing out on all the good things life has to offer.

The truth lies somewhere between nurture and nature. Don't become hard at heart or accept what your surroundings want to define you as. Don't allow how you were treated growing up to keep you from being the best you can be.

You are not meant to be a liar, but a truthful person. None of this is easy, as life is not easy.

Everyone must personally develop, accept, or resist their environment, regardless of the positive or negative impact, and the pain they may feel from it.

I know many people who have experienced the same environment growing up. They went down completely different paths in life and became quite opposites.

A minimally abusive home may cause you to accept, deny, or resist its effects. By accepting it, you risk becoming just like what you have accepted. Or you can deny it and potentially become something worse. In resisting it, you pledge to never be like that ever.

If you allow yourself to heal and to grow, you will be a good, non-abusive person. I'm not advocating abuse, ever!

Sometimes, the best resolution to the problem is evacuation, especially where there is abuse.

When dealing with the threat of an imminent tornado, some people may choose to stay and not evacuate, depending on its severity. While an EF1 or an EF2 tornado may not be viewed as very dangerous, an EF4 or EF5 tornado causes most rationally sane people to evacuate without hesitation.

It's the EF3 tornado that is the hardest to decide what to do during. Do I stay, or do I go?

Compared to abusive environments, some are difficult to determine if evacuation is the answer. In cases of minor abuse that is verbal, emotional, mental, and not at all physical or sexual, it can be understood if the parties involved want to stay and try to find a resolution.

Sometimes, we can't just leave the situation, as was in my case. I would never want to go through this abuse again in my life, as it was very painful and extremely unpleasant.

Through it, I developed the strength to resist and to fight it. I wanted to be more than that pain and not let it define me. I did not want to live a lie or give in.

There is a strength from resisting and from knowing when to leave. Staying too long when it is not safe will have the opposite impact. The damage it can cause is never worth the staying. Just find the strength to get out of there.

In my response to my environment, I decided to find forgiveness, not acceptance, as my abuser was more verbal and emotional than physical or sexual.

I'm appreciative of my environment for who I have become, though I believe there are much better ways to learn than through the pain of "Hard Knox."

My gratitude came from the process of changing, which is something we all have equally handed to us, regardless of nurture or nature.

Our choices and responses within each situation will determine who we will be. Many times, how we handle the pain in our life will impact how we manage pleasure.

For example, I appreciate that there was a bad example set for me with alcohol, but I am grateful that the process led me to moderation and then teetotalism.

I have come to appreciate who my father was and have found gratitude in the process that made me determined to be a better father. I appreciate my father's silence, which made me a talker, as well as his passiveness, which eventually made me assertive.

The darkness I had to deal with helped me appreciate the light. The loneliness I experienced gave me a desire for companionship, and the lack of self-awareness made me very aware.

Because I appreciate the past, does not mean that I agree with it, but it does mean that I acknowledge that it happened. I'm not hiding from it but exposing it. I'm not becoming like it but healing from it.

It could have all turned out differently. I could have chosen to be hard or just accept it. I didn't let it hold me back, I am moving forward.

You can resist it too. Develop the strength necessary to no longer live a lie but be the person you know you can be.

This all depends on you. Will you allow your pain and circumstances to define you and decide who you will be? Will you allow it to twist your identity and bring deception in your life? Will you embrace the lie and become a lair?

Or will you allow yourself to go through the process of

change and to be a new man in truth? Let there be gain from your pain.

Why Lie?

Reputation, credibility, honor, and trust all come from being true. Integrity is the result of a life that is based on truth.

How can you ever believe a liar or a fraud? It's pure insanity to think that you can pull an apple from an orange tree, or that you can drink fresh water from salty ocean water, without some sort of filter.

So why do you think you can trust a liar? You just can't! There is no honor among thieves and no honor among liars. They are the same.

Thieves steal and lie. Liars lie and steal something from you - trust. They also take away your dignity and respect, leaving you looking like a fool.

When a liar is exposed, they will blame others and take down anyone in their way.

Your credit score determines how financially trustworthy you are. When a company gives you a credit card, they are giving you access to money ahead of purchases. The intent is that you can be trusted to pay it back.

Yes, they make judgments about you financially, but otherwise, they would be giving you spending money with no rational way to recover it. They trust your past payment history and credit to determine their decision.

What credibility can you count on from a liar? Just like your credit score, in life, there is a character score, and people will judge you based on your "character" worthiness. What's your character score? Will you be trusted today based on your past performance and history?

You cannot expect people to take you at your word and to trust you when you are a liar and have no credibility at all and have a character score of zero.

You develop a reputation quickly based on the length of time that people have been able to believe in you or not believe in you. This determines what kind of reputation you will have to live with.

Once you gain a bad reputation, it is harder to change it than your bad behavior. If you live with the reputation of a liar, a cheat, or a fraud, no one will ever believe you.

Or you can live with the reputation of someone honest and true. People will listen to you, some will believe you, and everyone will benefit from your truth.

Men need to take regard for truth. Men have embraced so many lies that we have become a society of liars, cheats, and frauds.

Why would women like a man who lies when these men often don't even like themselves? We have become a disgrace to our culture and a stench. The world has turned their back on men that smell, men that lie.

Men who lie leave women to fend for themselves and pave their way in life alone, companionless. They leave children fatherless with no good examples to follow. They leave those they love bruised, hurting, and full of insecurity, all because men believed and became lies.

Boys, who band together in their lies, become worthless thugs with no credibility or honor. They are not men.

Society has turned its back on men because it has turned its back on liars. It's time for a change. It's time to embrace what is true. Now is the time for men everywhere to show the world what a real man can do and who a real man is. It's time to take back the definition of what it means to be a man.

The world can't refuse the actions of truthful men because he puts others first.

Men of honor know how to protect what is valuable. Men of credibility can be counted on. Men of love want what is best for others. Men of truth don't judge but accept. These men will make a difference because they have become the difference.

Men who fight for their family, care for others more than themselves, lift others when they are down, is who everyone around them wants to be like.

This is a man of truth. So, why do you lie?

Questions for Self-Reflection

How will being more committed change your relationships?

How will you stay accountable and to whom?

What wise decisions will help you to be persistent?

How will you increase your hunger for truth?

Who in your life can be the recipient of your positive truthful example?

WHY DO YOU LIE?

www.ingramcontent.com/pod-product-compliance
Lightning Source LLC
Chambersburg PA
CBHW071931150726
47999CB00001B/176